CLARENDON ANCIENT HISTORY SERIES

General Editors

Brian Bosworth   Miriam Griffin
David Whitehead

The aim of the CLARENDON ANCIENT HISTORY SERIES is to provide authoritative translations, introductions, and commentaries to a wide range of Greek and Latin texts studied by ancient historians. The books will be of interest to scholars, graduate students, and advanced undergraduates.

CORNELIUS NEPOS

A selection, including the lives of
CATO and ATTICUS

Translated
with Introductions and Commentary by

Nicholas Horsfall

CLARENDON PRESS · OXFORD
1989

Oxford University Press, Walton Street, Oxford OX2 6DP
Oxford New York Toronto
Delhi Bombay Calcutta Madras Karachi
Petaling Jaya Singapore Hong Kong Tokyo
Nairobi Dar es Salaam Cape Town
Melbourne Auckland
and associated companies in
Berlin Ibadan

Oxford is a trade mark of Oxford University Press

Published in the United States
by Oxford University Press, New York

British Library Cataloguing in Publication Data
Nepos, Cornelius
Cornelius Nepos: A selection, including the lives of
Cato and Atticus.—(Clarendon ancient history
series)
I. Title   II. Horsfall, Nicholas
878'.0108
ISBN 0–19–814903–4
ISBN 0–19–814915–8 (pbk)

Library of Congress Cataloging in Publication Data
Data available
ISBN 0–19–814903–4
ISBN 0–19–814915–8 (pbk)

Typset by Hope Services, Abingdon, Oxon
Printed in Great Britain by
Biddles Ltd, Guildford and King's Lynn

PREFACE

This collection includes Nepos' two Roman lives, the tiny *Cato* and the *Atticus*, with a collection of selected fragments of Cato, of Atticus, and of Nepos himself, which have never been gathered together and discussed in English. In addition, I translate and discuss Nepos' preface to his *Lives of the Foreign Generals*, central to our view of his cultural position and to his outlook as a biographer, and the 'Letter of Cornelia', transmitted with the works of Nepos, and engrossing in its own right. Elizabeth Rawson, in her book *Intellectual Life in the Late Roman Republic*, has done a very great deal to illuminate the byways of Roman history, biography, and antiquarian writing in the late republic, and a close look at some of the central texts may now be timely. It is possibly a consequence of a long-held conviction that 'Nepos is a school author' that he has never attracted scholars of distinction; commentaries on him have been of a lamentable standard for the most part, and it is my hope that this translation with commentary will make him more interesting and accessible: the *Atticus*, above all, is a central text which is only now emerging from millennia of neglect.

In recent months, I have occasionally been asked how, after my 'disdainful' remarks about Nepos in *CHCL* (p. xi quite falsely suggests other authorship of my bibl., 845), I could venture to return to an author I so little respected. To some elements of that condemnation I still adhere, unconvinced, for example, that Nepos writes elegant or agreeable Latin, and reluctant in my translation to conceal his lumbering periods behind discreet paraphrase. Elsewhere time has brought caution and revision (for example, on the *Chronica*). The *Atticus* was skimped in 1982, not least because it is in some ways a complex work which has quite literally never been studied right through in detail. To Nepos, as a biographer who is capable of trying honestly to hold up a mirror steadily to his subject, I shall hasten to pay tribute. Careful enquiry has, however, also revealed follies and vices hitherto unsuspected. Since my earlier discussion, a good deal has been written about Nepos: progress in research, therefore, has contributed actively to my rethinking, and the introductions will not be found to repeat much of the earlier treatment. For a bibliography of general discussions, though not much recommended, I refer to the first note to the Introduction; for the Latin text, I follow largely Marshall's Teubner edition; there is a loose English translation, which omits most of the fragments, in the Loeb series (see p. xv n. 1, s.v. Rolfe).

This commentary is not the work of a specialist historian, though I have previously ventured to discuss in detail some problems within the period. My original intention was to supply linguistic and literary notes to a commentary on the Latin text, in collaboration with an historian. That plan did not work out, and I am most grateful to the General Editors of this series for concluding that I could probably manage the whole thing on my own. David Miller first aroused my interest in the years 44–31 BC in 1961–2; many others, notably Erik Wistrand and Elizabeth Rawson, have encouraged me to keep looking at texts and problems which fall between specialists in history and literature.

I have tried not to persecute my friends with too many enquiries while writing this book, but am most gratefully aware of having written it with the learned and tolerant encouragement of Mariateresa Scotti and within the generously supporting environment of the Ashmolean Library, Oxford. At a late stage Elizabeth Rawson, Susan Treggiari, and Miriam Griffin exerted kindly vigilance. Above all, I have tried to recall what I learned from teaching Roman history to largely Latinless students at Macquarie University, New South Wales, in 1980. I shall be delighted if this book satisfies readers as demanding as they were, and even more so, if it meets the standards in friendship and scholarship of my colleague there Margaret Beattie, to whom I can only repeat what Catullus said to Nepos, 'quare habe tibi quidquid hoc libelli, qualecumque'.

7 July 1987   NICHOLAS HORSFALL

CONTENTS

BIBLIOGRAPHY AND ABBREVIATIONS

Standard abbreviations for authors, collections, and periodicals are in general not included here. For some works very frequently cited I have in the interests of concision used my own abbreviations, also listed below. For others, author and year alone are given in the text and full details may be found here. Neither all books cited only once or twice, nor any articles, with one or two exceptions, are listed here. I have tried to restrict the number of works not in English, wherever possible.

ANRW — H. Temporini and W. Haase (eds.), *Aufstieg und Niedergang der römischen Welt*, (Berlin 1972–   ).

Arnold (1914) — W. T. Arnold, *The Roman System of Provincial Administration* (Oxford 1914).

Astin (1967) — A. E. Astin, *Scipio Aemilianus* (Oxford 1967).

Astin (1978) — A. E. Astin, *Cato the Censor* (Oxford 1978).

Badian (1958) — E. Badian, *Foreign Clientelae 264–70 BC* (Oxford 1958)

Badian (1966) — E. Badian, 'The Early Historians' in T. A. Dorey (ed.), *The Latin Historians* (London 1966).

Badian (1972) — E. Badian, *Publicans and Sinners* (Oxford, Blackwell 1972).

Baldry (1965) — H. C. Baldry, *The Unity of Mankind in Greek Thought* (Cambridge 1965).

Balsdon (1962) — J. P. V. D. Balsdon, *Roman Women: Their History and Habits* (London 1962).

Balsdon (1969) — J. P. V. D. Balsdon, *Life and Leisure in Ancient Rome* (London 1969).

Balsdon (1979) — J. P. V. D. Balsdon, *Romans and Aliens* (London 1979).

Bernstein (1978) — A. H. Bernstein, *Tiberius Sempronius Gracchus: Tradition and Apostasy* (Ithaca 1978).

Bickerman (1968) — E. J. Bickerman, *Chronology of the Ancient World* (London 1968).

Bonner (1977) S. F. Bonner, *Education in Ancient Rome* (London 1977).

Bremmer and Horsfall (1987) J. N. Bremmer and N. M. Horsfall, *Roman Myth and Mythography*, *BICS* Suppl. 51 (1987).

Brunt (1965) P. A. Brunt, 'Amicitia in the Late Roman Republic', *PCPhS* 11 (1965), 1 ff. = Seager (1969), 199 ff.

Brunt (1971) P. A. Brunt, *Social Conflicts in the Roman Republic* (London 1971).

Byrne (1920) A. H. Byrne, *Titus Pomponius Atticus: Chapters of a Biography* (Lancaster, Pa. 1920).

CHCL *Cambridge History of Classical Literature*, vol. ii: *Latin Literature* (Cambridge 1982).

CIL *Corpus Inscriptionum Latinarum.*

Crook (1967) J. A. Crook, *Law and Life of Rome* (London 1967).

D'Alton (1917) J. F. D'Alton, *Horace and his Age* (London 1917).

D'Arms (1970) J. H. D'Arms, *Romans on the Bay of Naples* (Cambridge, Mass. 1970).

D'Arms (1981) J. H. D'Arms, *Commerce and Social Standing in Ancient Rome* (Cambridge, Mass. 1981).

Davies (1971) J. K. Davies, *Athenian Propertied Families* (Oxford 1971).

Douglas (1966) A. E. Douglas (ed.), *Cicero*: Brutus (Oxford 1966).

Dover (1980) K. J. Dover, *Greek Homosexuality* (New York 1980).

Drumann W. Drumann, *Geschichte Roms*, 2nd edn., rev. P. Groebe (Berlin–Leipzig 1899–).

ESAR T. Frank (ed.), *Economic Survey of Ancient Rome* (Baltimore 1933–).

Finley (1973) M. I. Finley, *The Ancient Economy* (London 1973).

Friedlaender L. Friedlaender, *Roman Life and Manners* tr. L. A. Magnus, J. H. Freese, 4 vols. (London 1908–13).

Garnsey (1976) P. D. A. Garnsey, 'Urban Property Investment', in M. I. Finley (ed.), *Studies in Roman Property*, (Cambridge 1976).

Geiger (1985) J. Geiger, *Cornelius Nepos and Ancient*

Political Biography, Hermes Einzelschr. 47 (Stuttgart 1985).

Gelzer (1969) — M. Gelzer, *The Roman Nobility*, tr. R. Seager (Oxford, Blackwell 1969).

Griffin (1985) — J.Griffin, *Latin Poets and Roman Life* (Oxford 1985).

Gruen (1974) — E. S. Gruen, *The Last Generation of the Roman Republic* (Berkeley 1974).

Guthrie (1969) — W. K. C. Guthrie, *History of Greek Philosophy*, iii (London 1969).

Hallett (1984) — J. P. Hallett, *Fathers and Daughters in Roman Society* (Princeton 1984).

Hellegouarc'h (1963) — J. Hellegouarc'h, *Le Vocabulaire latin des relations et des partis politiques* (Paris 1963/ 1972; reprinted with identical pagination).

Hill (1952) — H. Hill, *The Roman Middle Class in the Republican Period* (Oxford 1952).

HRR — *Historicorum Romanorum reliquiae*, ed. H. Peter, i² (Leipzig 1914), ii (Leipzig 1906).

Jal (1963) — P. Jal, *La Guerre civile à Rome* (Paris 1963).

Kaimio (1979) — J. Kaimio, *The Romans and the Greek Language* (Comm. hum. lit. 64), (Helsinki 1979).

Keaveney (1982) — A. Keaveney, *Sulla: The Last Republican* (London 1982).

Kennedy (1972) — G. Kennedy, *The Art of Rhetoric in the Roman World* (Princeton 1982).

Lacey (1968) — W. K. Lacey, *The Family in Classical Greece* (London 1968).

Lazenby (1978) — J. F. Lazenby, *Hannibal's War* (Warminster 1978).

Leo (1901) — F. Leo, *Die griechisch-römische Biographie* (Leipzig 1901).

Lewis and Reinhold — N. Lewis and M. Reinhold, *Roman Civilisation*, 2 vols. (New York 1966).

Lintott (1968) — A. W. Lintott, *Violence in Republican Rome* (Oxford 1968).

Macleod (1983) — C. W. Macleod, *Collected Essays* (Oxford 1983).

Marrou (1956) — H.-I. Marrou, *A History of Education in Antiquity*, tr. G. Lamb (London 1956).

Marshall — I translate the text of P. K. Marshall, *C.*

Nepotis vitae cum fragmentis (Leipzig 1977), except on the occasions (indicated) where I doubt that he prints what N. wrote.

Michell (1952)   H. Michell, *Sparta* (Cambridge 1952).

Mitchell (1979)   T. N. Mitchell, *Cicero: The Ascending Years* (New Haven 1979).

Momigliano (1971)   A. D. Momigliano, *The Development of Greek Biography* (Cambridge, Mass. 1971).

MRR   T. R. S. Broughton, *Magistrates of the Roman Republic*, 2 vols. (New York 1951, 1952).

N.   Cornelius Nepos (no *praenomen* is preserved).

Nicolet (1966), (1974)   C. Nicolet, *L'Ordre équestre à l'époque républicaine*, Bibl. Ec. Fr. Ath. Rome 207, 2 vols. (Paris 1966, 1974).

Nicolet (1980)   *The World of the Citizen in Republican Rome*, tr. P. Falla (London 1980).

OCD²   *Oxford Classical Dictionary*, 2nd edn. (Oxford 1970).

Ogilvie (1965)   *A Commentary on Livy 1–5* (Oxford 1965).

ORF²   *Oratorum Romanorum fragmenta*, ed. H. Malcovati, 2nd edn. (Turin 1955).

Petrochilos (1974)   N. K. Petrochilos, *Roman Attitudes to the Greeks* (Athens 1974).

Pomeroy (1975)   S. B. Pomeroy, *Goddesses, Wives, Whores, and Slaves* (New York 1975).

Ramage (1973)   E. S. Ramage, *Urbanitas: Ancient Sophistication and Refinement* (Norman, Okla., 1973).

Rawson (1969)   E. Rawson, *The Spartan Tradition in European Thought* (Oxford 1969).

Rawson (1975)   E. Rawson, *Cicero: A Portrait* (London 1975).

Rawson (1985)   E. Rawson, *Intellectual Life in the Late Roman Republic* (London 1985).

Rice Holmes   T. Rice Holmes, *The Roman Republic*, 3 vols. (London 1923).

RH, ARE   T. Rice Holmes, *The Architect of the Roman Empire*, 2 vols. (London 1928, 1931).

Richardson (1986)   J. S. Richardson, *Hispaniae: Spain and the Development of Roman Imperialism* (Cambridge 1986).

Rostovtzeff (1953)	M. I. Rostovtzeff, *Social and Economic History of the Hellenistic World*, 3 vols. (repr. Oxford 1953–9).
Saller (1982)	R. P. Saller, *Personal Patronage under the Early Empire* (Cambridge 1982).
SB i, etc.	Cicero, *Letters to Atticus*, ed. D. R. Shackleton Bailey, 7 vols. (Cambridge 1965–70).
SB *Fam.*	Cicero, *Epistulae ad familiares*, ed. D. R. Shackleton Bailey, 2 vols. (Cambridge 1977).
SB *QF, Brut.*	Cicero, *Epistolae ad Quintum fratrem, ad M. Brutum*, ed. D. R. Shackleton Bailey (Cambridge 1980).
Schanz–Hosius	M. Schanz, *Geschichte der römischen Literatur*, i⁴, rev. C. Hosius (Munich 1927).
Scullard (1973)	H. H. Scullard, *Roman Politics 220–150 BC*, 2nd edn. (Oxford 1973).
Seager (1969)	R. Seager (ed.), *The Crisis of the Roman Republic* (Cambridge, Heffer 1969).
Shatzman (1975)	I. Shatzman, *Senatorial Wealth and Roman Politics*, Coll. Latomus 142 (Brussels 1975).
Skutsch (1985)	*The* Annals *of Quintus Ennius*, ed. O. Skutsch (Oxford 1985).
Steidle (1951)	W. Steidle, *Sueton und die antike Biographie*, Zetemata 1 (Munich 1951).
Sumner (1973)	G. V. Sumner, *Orators in Cicero's* Brutus (Toronto 1973).
Suolahti (1955)	J. Suolahti, *Junior Officers of the Roman Army*, Ann. Acad. Scient. Fenn. Ser. B 97 (Helsinki 1955).
Syme (1939)	R. Syme, *The Roman Revolution* (Oxford 1939).
Ross Taylor (1931)	L. Ross Taylor, *The Divinity of the Roman Emperor* (Middletown, Conn. 1931).
Ross Taylor (1964)	L. Ross Taylor, *Party Politics in the Age of Caesar* (Berkeley 1949, reprinted 1964).
Teuffel	W. S. Teuffel, *Geschichte der römischen Literatur*, i⁶ (much revised, Berlin 1916).
Treggiari (1969)	S. Treggiari, *Roman Freedmen in the Late Republic* (Oxford 1969).
Wallace-Hadrill (1983)	A. Wallace-Hadrill, *Suetonius: The Scholar and his* Caesars (London 1983).

Watson (1967)	A. Watson, *The Law of Persons in the Later Roman Republic* (Oxford 1967).
Weinstock (1971)	S. Weinstock, *Divus Iulius* (Oxford 1971).
Willetts (1965)	R. F. Willetts, *Ancient Crete: A Social History* (London 1965).
Wiseman (1971)	T. P. Wiseman, *New Men in the Roman Senate 139 BC–AD 14* (Oxford 1971).
Wiseman (1979)	T. P. Wiseman, *Clio's Cosmetics* (Leicester 1979).
Wiseman (1985)	T. P. Wiseman, *Catullus and his World: A Reappraisal* (Cambridge 1985).
Wistrand (1978)	E. Wistrand, *Caesar and Contemporary Roman Society* (Göteborg 1978).
Wistrand (1981)	E. Wistrand, *The Policy of Brutus the Tyrannicide* (Göteborg 1981).

Addendum

Between submission of my MS and the arrival of the proofs, some little while elapsed; my researches revealed omissions, while other students of N. have also been unusually active: large new books on Agrippa (Roddaz) and Roman banking (Andreau) add little. Fergus Millar has used N.'s *Atticus* to illustrate many aspects of the transition from Republic to Empire (*G & R* 35 (1988), 40–55), while A. C. Dionisotti (*JRS* 78 (1988), 35–49) studies the possible contemporary and programmatic significance of N.'s *Greek Generals*, without reinforcing her conclusions by means of analogies with the *Atticus*. M. Labate and E. Narducci ('Mobilità dei modelli etici . . . il 'personaggio' di Attico' in A. Giardina and A. Schiavone, (eds.) *Società romana e produzione schiavistica* 3 (Rome 1981), 127–82, 382–402) study N.'s ideology in great depth, where I see little more than careful reading of Cicero and absorption of a few current prejudices! Some of the papers of P. A. Brunt that I cite have now been collected (much altered) in his *Fall of the Roman Republic* (Oxford 1988), as have those of Peter Wiseman in *Roman Studies* (Liverpool 1987). To our understanding of the literary tradition about the elder Cato Jonathan Powell's edition of Cicero's *De senectute* contributes a good deal, as did Jane Stuart-Smith to my ability to survive the ordeal of publication.

Ravello
12 March 1989

GENERAL INTRODUCTION

Nepos[1] was born about 110 BC,[2] a Transpadane, from perhaps Pavia or Milan: he was clearly interested in the geography of the Po valley,[3] and it is possible that the fragments of geographical content which N.'s latest editor Marshall lumps together with the *Exempla* (for which cf. p. xvii–xviii), actually belong to a separate geographical work whose very title we have lost.[4] The poet Catullus, from Verona and twenty-five years N.'s junior, shared N.'s interest in their homeland (4, 17, 31, 39. 13, etc.):[5] the literary compliments that passed between them we shall have to discuss in more detail (p. 117).

N. is not attested at Rome before 65 BC (see note on fr. 38), the year in which he says Atticus came back from Greece (*Att.* 4. 5). There is not a word of any political activities or interests, though he speaks bravely of Mark Antony and with no warmth of Octavian (see note on *Att.* 20. 5, prizes); his moralizing about the evils of the present is conventional and traditional, and lies quite outside any definable political affiliations (see notes on *Cato*, 2. 2, law, and *Att.* 6. 2, traditional manner).

It is not clear to me whether he met Cicero or Atticus first; fragment 37 (see accompanying note) might suggest that as early as 80 BC he did not know Cicero,[6] and in 65 they were not necessarily acquainted (*supra*). The 'circle of the Villa Tamphiliana' (Atticus' town house; cf. note on *Att.* 13. 2, Tamphilus') can be made to sound like a research seminar in history and antiquities for gentleman amateurs,[7] where N., Atticus, Cicero, and Varro thrashed out the facts about the Roman past. Atticus very clearly was partial to historical

---

[1] General treatments of N.: apart from mine (Horsfall, *CHCL*) cf. first the old handbooks, Schanz–Hosius, i. 351 ff., Teuffel, i. 455 ff., PW iv. 1408 f. (by G. Wissowa). See Geiger (1985), 66 ff.; Rawson (1985), 230 f. *et passim*; Wiseman (1979), 154 ff. There is also a Loeb translation of all the lives and a few fragments (with Florus) by J. C. Rolfe (London 1929 etc.).

[2] *Att.* 19. 1: N. talks as though he and Atticus were roughly contemporaries.

[3] e.g. Geiger (1985), 67 n. 1.

[4] Frr. 18, 19, 20, 23 Marshall; Geiger (1985), 67 n. 2, 72 f., 109.

[5] Wiseman (1985), 107 ff.   [6] Cf. J. Geiger, *Lat.* 44 (1985), 262.

[7] Momigliano (1971), 97; E. Jenkinson, *ANRW* i. 3, 704.

discussion (*Att.* 18, 20 n. 3), but there is no hint to suggest that N. went there as early as 60 (say) at all regularly, nor that Varro was specially intimate with Atticus.[8] Literary 'circles' are easier to invent than to prove;[9] N.'s place in Roman cultural life is not easy to define.

Particularly, it is hard to measure the tone and temper of his relations with Cicero.[10] If N. said openly that Cicero's philosophical works were 'not worth reading', and told him that philosophy was not the 'mistress of life' (fr. 39 with note),[11] there must have been difficulties. On the other hand, two books of Cicero's letters to him were preserved,[12] he paid ample tribute to Cicero's eloquence and potential as a historian (fr. 58), wrote his life in at least two books, and perhaps helped prepare other Ciceronian letters for publication. But not a word of Cicero's death in the *Atticus*. I draw no conclusions. The great polymath Varro N. must have known,[13] but there is no evidence for social or intellectual rapport. The provincial N. never aspired to a public career, and had no appetite for Varro's application of prodigious but wayward learning to the distant Roman past. We shall see that they·covered many of the same topics but there is no evidence even for contact, let alone friendship. My description of N. as an 'intellectual pygmy' attracted a good deal of amused opprobrium:[14] without doubt, though, he was the social and intellectual inferior of Varro, Atticus, and Cicero.

N.'s literary output has often been listed and studied: I shall do so again briefly. Two superficially conflicting features I shall try to illuminate in passing are, first, his consistent

---

[8] E. Rawson, *JRS* 62 (1972), 33 ff. SB on Cic. *Att.* 2. 20. 1 perhaps overstates the degree of friendship; cf. Drumann, 82. Intellectually, the two men were extremely different (cf. p. 0 f.).

[9] Cf. Astin (1967), 294 ff.

[10] Gell. 15. 28. 1 is acknowledged by all to be exaggerated and of little evidential value. At *Lat.* 44 (1985), 261 ff. J. Geiger offers overheated polemic: on any interpretation, Cic. *Att.* 16. 5. 5 is a joke at N.'s expense shared by Cicero and Atticus. Further details summarized: J. Geiger, *Lat.* 44 (1985), 261 ff.; Horsfall, *CHCL* 290.

[11] Cic. loc. cit., with SB's note; J. Geiger, *Lat.* 44 (1985), 264. But Tyrrell and Purser (5. 379) interpret Cic. differently. Cf. A. Setaioli, *Symb. Osl.* 51 (1976), 105 ff. for a sceptical view of the date Cicero's letters were published.

[12] J. Geiger, *Lat.* 44 (1985), 264 ff.; ib., 270 for N.'s possible role as editor of Cicero.

[13] Horsfall, *CHCL* 286 ff.; Rawson (1985), 235 ff.

[14] Horsfall, *CHCL* ii 290. Cf. T. P. Wiseman, *History*, 218 (1981), 375–93, *passim*.

appetite for topics in tune with current tastes and interests, and, secondly, his 'originality', which has attracted a good deal of attention recently (see note on fr. 2 of *Chronica*):

(i) Love-poetry: a very common pastime among educated Romans of the age, and not to be taken seriously as a possible foundation of the good relations between N. and Catullus.

(ii) Biographies, both long (Cicero, *supra*, and the elder Cato, in one book, see note on *Cato*, 3. 5, separate study) and short (the *De viris illustribus* (On Distinguished Men of which *Cato*, *Atticus*, and the book *Lives of the Foreign Generals* survive) will be discussed in greater detail in my introduction to the *Atticus* (p. 10–11); we shall find both that there was a great deal of writing of a biographical character in the 40s, and that N. may possibly have priority in both types.

(iii) Relative chronology, that is to say, in the cultural and political history of Greece and Rome simultaneously. N. writes *Chronica* (p. 31–2); they were shortly to be superseded by Atticus' own *liber annalis* (cf. p. 39–40), which strongly influenced Cicero. N. clearly has formal priority.

(iv) Geographical phenomena, on which there may have been a separate work (cf. p. xv); Varro too wrote a *Fundanius de admirandis*, 'on marvels', and Cicero a lost *Admiranda* (cf. note on *Cato*, 3. 4, events and sights on the role of *admiranda* in Cato's *Origines*).[15]

(v) Literary terminology (fr. 61, p. 120); a deeply mysterious lost pamphlet whose content may well have resembled much that is preserved in Varro.[16]

(vi) *Exempla*, moral examples, in at least five books; only twice attested explicitly (frr. 10, 12 Marshall), but it is likely that at least the fragments of N. preserved by the elder Pliny on topics connected with the history of luxury at Rome should be attributed to it. The very large collection of *exempla* by Valerius Maximus, writing under Tiberius, gives us perhaps some idea of what N.'s collection may have been like. N.'s *Exempla* were indeed the first such collection of which we know at Rome.[17] The subject-matter, though (cf. fr. 62, p. 34; not

---

[15] Geiger (1985), 72 n. 37.
[16] Cf. Rawson (1985), 117 ff.
[17] G. Maslakov, *ANRW* ii. 32. 1, 437 ff., 457 ff.; Geiger (1985), 72 ff.

just trivia about the history of luxury;[18] cf. Gell. 6. 18. 2, 19. 1), is familiar: Cato's history 'in large letters' (see note on *Cato*, 3. 2, histories) was explicitly exemplary in intent, and rhetoricians before Cicero, were already discussing the use of the *exemplum*.[19] But it is N. who apparently identifies the need and makes the first actual collection.

It looks repeatedly as though N. has an exceptional talent for seeing what was lacking, and would prove a useful and attractive topic, even if we cannot be sure that he always wrote for the same audience group: that of the *De viris illustribus* is at once identifiable and elusive (pp. xix–xxi), but we cannot assume that the *Chronica* were aimed at the same level. He will have merited thanks for his industry, not admiration for his genius. His feeble appetite for exactitude and primary sources, for archival research and the Greek language[20] cannot have inspired respect among those qualified to judge. There is an interesting paradox here: N.'s energies clearly outstrip his talents; put another way, though he is full of good ideas, he not only fails to execute them with care or skill, but alienates readers by his poor Latin.

In his great survey of prose style from the sixth century BC to the Renaissance, Eduard Norden delivered a ringing condemnation of N. as a writer,[21] to which there has been (and can be) no real answer. N. wrote a vast amount, yet very clearly had no serious grounding in how to use his own language. He does not aim to write the Latin of Cicero, and should not be judged by Ciceronian standards; the trouble is more basic. He has mastered only a very few rhetorical devices and flogs them, on almost every page, to death: antitheses, a very limited development of sentence structure, monotonous alliteration, inadequate mastery of the basic principles of prose rhythm and word order. Thus far Norden.

---

[18] Fr. 27, beginning with 'when I was a boy . . .': changes in the fashion for various kinds of purple; fr. 28: when did the Romans begin to fatten thrushes?; fr. 31: before Sulla's victory there were only two silver dinner couches at Rome; fr. 33: the first man to put marble veneer on his walls; fr. 34: on the fashion for wine-jars of onyx.

[19] Cf. G. Maslakov, *ANRW* ii. 32. 1, 439 n. 5; H. W. Litchfield, *HSCP* 25 (1914), 6 ff.

[20] Cf. Rawson (1985), 231; Horsfall, *CHCL*, 292; *Athen.* 65 (1987), 232; E. Jenkinson, *ANRW* i. 3, 713 ff.

[21] *Antike Kunstprosa*, i⁵ (repr. Darmstadt 1958), 204 ff.

I would add a limited, trite, and repetitive vocabulary,[22] and would stress even more than Norden does that when N. attempts a longer or more elaborate sentence (e.g. 12. 5, 14. 2, 20. 5, where I hope that the translation reflects something of the original's awkwardness), both structure and coherence falter.

Since the Renaissance[23] N. has regularly, and throughout Europe, been used as a school author. The plainness of his style and the intensity of his moral tone (cf. notes on *Att.* 1. 2, in all and 5. 1, devotion) will have endeared him to educators, and they evidently outweighed his historical inaccuracy (more clearly visible in the *Cato* and the *Foreign Generals* than in the *Atticus*) and stylistic ineptitude. Yet voices were raised in protest: one Harnow, in Germany in 1850, in his essay 'on removing Nepos from the place he holds in the schools', wrote that 'he is to be kept away from boys of twelve like the plague'.[24] But the *Atticus* is by far the best thing he did to survive, and the deficiencies of his Latin are inevitably mitigated in translation.

The paradox of N.'s unequal interests and abilities is better understood if we look, lastly, at the public for which he tells us most explicitly, in the *Foreign Generals*, that he is writing. N. writes for a public 'expertes Graecarum litterarum' (*Praef.* 2), who have no Greek, and for those 'rudibus Graecarum litterarum', 'innocent of Greek letters' (*Pelop.* 16. 1). He will have to go into detail to explain what a great man Pelopidas was. He has to interpret Greek terms (cf. note on *Att.* 2. 6, medimnus), or render Greek terms by Latin equivalents,[25] to explain Greek *mores* to Roman readers unfamiliar with them,[26] who may be expected to disapprove; and to explain the historical background to the *Foreign Generals* to an audience who could not read the Greek historians and therefore knew

---

[22] Norden notes that the language of Atticus' final speech (21. 5–6) is in a 'quite vulgar tone': this might confirm my suggestion that N. had not been present and was relying on reports (see note on this section, health).

[23] Cf. M. L. Clarke, *Classical Education in Britain, 1500–1900* (Cambridge 1959), 194 f.

[24] Cf. F. A. Eckstein, *Lateinischer und griechischer Unterricht* (Leipzig 1887), 209 f.

[25] *Imperator* or *praetor* for *strategos*, *senatus* for *gerusia*, *praefectus* for satrap: Horsfall, *CHCL* 292; E. Jenkinson, *ANRW*, i. 3, 712 f.

[26] There is no adequte discussion in English: but cf. W. M. Seaman, *CJ* 50 (1954–5), 115 ff.; C. Knapp, *AJPh* 40 (1919), 231 ff.; J. N. Hough, *AJPh* 55 (1934), 346 ff.

nothing of history beyond the Adriatic (*Pelop.* 1. 1). It is very striking that Plautus' audience, one hundred and fifty years before, appears to have been far more casually bilingual, and to have been amused, not outraged, by cultural differences (see notes of *Praef.* 2–5, *Epam.* 1. 1–3). Much of Plautus' fun with Greek mythology depends on familiarity (derived usually from the tragic stage) with the 'straight' version. In the first century BC, the hugely popular Mime poked fun at Greek philosophy.[27] Cicero was not amused: neither poet nor audience knew their letters.[28]

Modern readers of Latin literature are used to studying texts which presuppose familiarity with Greek as well (Catullus, Virgil, Horace, for example). N.'s audience is far more elusive,[29] and we cannot quite safely assume that the needs of the audience of the *Chronica* were those of the readers of the *De viris illustribus*.[30] Translations from the Greek might serve to identify these readers more fully, but when Cicero translated Aratus' *Phaenomena* or Xenophon's *Oeconomicus*, he did so principally to improve his Greek and Latin style;[31] Varro of Atax' version of Apollonius of Rhodes' *Argonautica* was sophisticated Latin Alexandrianism.[32] The *Iliads* of Matius and Ninnius Crassus may, however, have been closer to the modern popularizing translation in intent, and Cicero tells us quite explicitly that literal translations of Greek drama did exist (*Fin.* 1. 4).[33]

N. refers to Homer, *Iliad* 2. 204 (*Dion* 6. 4) but in such a way

---

[27] Cf. Rawson (1985), 53; Horsfall, *CHCL* 293.

[28] Cf. F. Giancotti, *Mimo e gnome* (Florence 1967), 119 ff., citing a fragment of Cicero's lost *Pro Gallio*.

[29] Geiger (1985), 95 f.; Rawson (1985), 49 f. A.-M. Guillemin's discussion of 'les demi-cultivés' in her *Le Public et la vie littéraire à Rome* (Paris 1937), 18 ff. is interesting but does not touch on N.

[30] Geiger (1985), 70 suggests stimulatingly that the *Chronica* might have appealed to a public perplexed by how Homer, Archilochus, and the Olympic Games might fit into a chronological scheme that they could themselves comprehend. Those are not the grounds on which the originality of the *Chronica* is now advanced by its more ardent admirers (cf. note on *Praef.* 8, haste). But if the public of *De viris illustribus* and *Chronica* really were the same, then Geiger is surely right. He compares the public of Velleius: cf. R. J. Starr, *CQ* 31 (1981), 173 f.

[31] Cf. Horsfall, *EMC* 23 (1979), 83 f.

[32] Cf. W. V. Clausen, *Virgil's Aeneid and Hellenistic Poetry* (Berkeley 1987), 5.

[33] H. D. Jocelyn, *Tragedies of Ennius* (Cambridge 1967), 26 f.; D. M. Jones, *BICS* 6 (1959), 28.

that the Greekless reader would have no trouble, and similarly to Xenophon's *Agesilaus* (*Ages.* 1. 1; cf. p. 10 for this work). But his own Greek is weak, and clearly none is presupposed in his readers.

Geiger interestingly compares the intended readership of some of Cicero's philosophical works;[34] Cicero knew that there was a public potentially interested in philosophy, which was put off because the primary language of philosophical discussion was Greek (*Ac.* 1. 4, 10; *ND* 1. 8; *Fin.* 1. 10; *Tusc.* 5. 116):[35] hence his pioneering work in Latin.[36] 'Even artisans enjoy history', he wrote (*Fin.* 5. 2).[37] But what artisan had the time to read, or the money to buy N.? Four hundred lives, we may remember, at from three pages upwards.[38] But the very existence of the *De viris illustribus* proves that there was a public ignorant but curious, Greekless but leisured, prosperous yet gullible. N. is at the heart of an insoluble problem of cultural history.

[34] Geiger (1985), 70 f.

[35] Horsfall, *EMC* 23 (1979), 88; Rawson (1985), 48.

[36] The few 'proto-Epicureans' hardly signify: cf. note on Nepos, fr. 58; Rawson (1985), 48 f.

[37] Rawson (1985), 49; Geiger (1985), 71; A.-M. Guillemin, *Le Public*, collects a number of passages (10 ff.: Cic. *De or.* 2. 338, 3. 198, *Brut.* 200, *Orat.* 173) where Cicero pays compliments to the acuteness of ear and rhetorical taste of the audience for public speeches at Rome.

[38] Cf. Rawson (1985), 44: the cost of books remains a mystery at this date. Cf. p. 11 n. 19 for the scale of the work.

TRANSLATIONS

LIFE OF CATO

N. has set himself an arguably difficult and probably uncongenial task.[1] The longer life (now lost) of Cato, the orator, historian, general, moralist, and farmer, who glowers down to us from his dominant position in the Roman history of 200–150 BC, appears to have been a success, but Cato clearly also had to have a place in the *De viris illustribus*, N.'s huge biographical handbook (p. 11). Where? Neither among Roman generals nor among Latin orators would he have been out of place, but N. chose to set him among the historians,[2] where, given that the *Origines* were the first work of narrative history in Latin, he perhaps above all belonged. This was the thirteenth or perhaps fourteenth book of the eighteen books of the *De viris illustribus*.[3]

A swift summary, therefore, of the longer work, with an appropriate cross-reference, and an emphasis on the subject's historical output, which we might compare with chapter 18 of the *Atticus*. Of the extant lives only the *Reges*, *Iphicrates*, and *Aristides* are shorter; *Chabrias* is the same length. N. wrote (p. xvi) a life of Cicero in several books; there was also a clearly much shorter version in the *De viris illustribus*, again misattributed by the manuscript to the *Latin Historians*, but most probably belonging to the *Latin Orators*.[4] (For the *Latin Historians* cf. also frr. 56 and 57 (p. 33).)

It is easy enough to see what N. could have used by way of source material for the *Cato*,[5] almost impossible to prove what he actually did use.

Hannibal 13. 1 suggests acquaintance with Polybius, also cited by Plutarch in his life of the elder Cato (10. 3). Plutarch (17. 5) also cites Cicero, *De senectute*: a remarkable portrait of Cato and a work which, it will emerge independently, N. had studied (see note on *Att.* 4. 1, captured). N. refers to Cato's partners as aedile, consul, and censor (1. 3, 2. 1, 2. 3); this was not arcane information, but the last two items were available in Atticus' *Liber annalis* (see note on *Att.* 18. 1, volume). Cicero (*Brut.* 65) mentions over one hundred and

---

[1] This has been missed by the authors of our standard discussions of Latin epitomes; but cf. Woodman, *CQ* 25 (1975), 272 ff. for some fine observations on the epitome in general.

[2] Hardly three lives of Cato! Cf. J. Geiger, *Lat.* 38 (1979), 666.

[3] Gell. 11. 8. 5; cf. note on Nepos. fr. 58, Albinus; Geiger (1985), 84 ff., 87; id., *Lat.* 38 (1979), 662 ff.

[4] Cf. p. 125 and Geiger (1985), 89.

[5] Astin (1978), 299 f.

fifty extant speeches by Cato.[6] Gellius (13. 20. 17) refers to a 'liber commentarius de familia Porcia'. N. himself (see 1. 1 with note, was . . . relating) mentions oral tradition. There are numerous references (Cic. *Off.* 1. 37; Plut. *Cat. mai.* 20. 10) to Cato's surviving letters.[7] Nor of course were annalists' accounts of the years of Cato's life lacking. But what N. did in the face of this mass of material, we have no idea.[8] The summary of the *Origines* (3. 3–4) is in part a shambles. We shall never know whether the longer version was better. The deficiencies probably reflect only hasty and unverified abbreviation; that he at least glanced at the original we can hardly deny. Other weaknesses may be inherited by N. from the year-by-year chronicles of his annalistic sources.[9] He elects neither to quote nor to paraphrase the Censor's words (but cf. note on 2. 3, sprout, on the metaphor *pullulare*); the remarkable flavour of the man himself never therefore really emerges. Contrast, on a similar scale, John Aubrey's *Brief Lives*;[10] take even lives of men who died over a century before Aubrey wrote.[11] The comparison, even if we make all allowance for the tedious necessities of abbreviation under which N. laboured, does not do him great credit, given the remarkable personality of his subject.

[6] Astin (1978), 133 ff.; cf. p. 35.
[7] Cf. P. Cugusi, *Epistolographi Latini Minores*, i. 65 ff.
[8] The terms of the laudation at 3. 1 recur at Plin. *NH* 7. 100 and Liv. 39. 40. 4, but are too general to encourage conclusions about consultation of N. or common sources.
[9] Notably the origins of the feud with Scipio and the account of Scipio's consulate; cf. note on 1. 3 (life). See Badian (1966), 2 ff.
[10] The Penguin edition by Oliver Lawson Dick has been reprinted many times.
[11] Bonner; Colet; Erasmus; William Herbert, first Earl of Pembroke; More; Sidney; Wolsey.

(**1. 1**) Marcus Cato, a native of the town of Tusculum, as a young man, before he gave his attention to a public career, lived in Sabinum, because he owned an estate there, left him by his father. Then encouraged by Lucius Valerius Flaccus, who was his colleague as consul and censor, as Marcus Perperna the ex-censor was fond of relating, he went to settle in Rome and began to take part in public life. (**1. 2**) He served his first campaign at the age of seventeen. In the consulship of Q. Fabius and M. Claudius, he was military tribune in Sicily. When he returned, he joined the staff of C. Claudius Nero and his services in the battle of Sena, where Hasdrubal the brother of Hannibal was killed, were valued highly. (**1. 3**) As quaestor he was allotted to P. Africanus, the consul, with whom he did not live in keeping with the bond of the lot, for he disagreed with him all his life. He was made plebeian aedile together with Gaius Helvius. As praetor, he secured Sardinia as his province; (**1. 4**) it was from Sardinia that he had as quaestor on an earlier occasion, on his way back from Africa, brought home Quintus Ennius the poet: that we value no less highly than the greatest triumph for achievements in Sardinia.

(**2. 1**) He held the consulship with L. Valerius Flaccus, was allotted Hither Spain as his province and from it bore home a triumph. (**2. 2**) When he stayed in Spain rather too long, Publius Scipio Africanus, whose quaestor Cato had been in his first consulship, when consul for the second time, wanted to remove him from his province and succeed him in person; this he was not able to achieve through the senate, though Scipio did occupy the leading position in the state, because at that time the republic was governed not by power but by the rule of law. He was as a result angry with the senate and when his consulship was over, remained in Rome, holding no office. (**2. 3**) But Cato, elected censor together with the L. Valerius Flaccus already mentioned, wielded that office with severity. For he both took action against numerous nobles and added many new items to the edict, in order that luxury, which was already beginning to sprout might be repressed. (**2. 4**) For about eighty years, from his youth right up to the end of his life, he never stopped taking on feuds for the sake of the republic. Many assailed him, yet not only did he lose nothing of his reputation, but, so long as he lived, grew in the admiration his virtues attracted.

(**3. 1**) He was in all respects exceptionally hard-working: for he was a skilled farmer, an expert lawyer, a great general, a convincing orator, and a great lover of literature: (**3. 2**) though he only seized upon the pursuit of letters as an older man, yet he made such progress that it is hard to find anything in Greek or Italian affairs that he did not know. (**3. 3**) From his early manhood he composed speeches; as an old man he began to write histories: seven books survive. The first contains the deeds of the kings of the Roman people, the second and third the origins of all the communities of Italy; in consequence he seems to have called the whole work *Origines*. In the fourth occurs the first Punic war, in the fifth, the second. (**3. 4**) All this is related summarily. The remaining wars he recounts in the same way down to the praetorship of Servius Galba, who pillaged the Lusitanians. He did not mention the generals in these wars by name, but recorded the facts without names. In the same work, he related the notable events and sights in both Italy and Spain. The work shows much industry and diligence, but no learning. (**3. 5**) I have written further about Cato's life and character in my separate study on him, made at the request of Titus Pomponius Atticus. So I refer those interested in him to that work.

LIFE OF ATTICUS

N.'s life of Atticus is without question by far the best of his works to survive, and it is the only one to treat a contemporary: T. Pomponius Atticus, intimate friend of Cicero, recipient of the sixteen books surviving of Cicero's *Letters to Atticus*, knight, neutral, banker, fixer, survivor, and also a scholar of exceptional care and accuracy. N.'s acquaintance with him is hard to define: they could even have met through Cicero, and Atticus was the dedicatee at least of the book on Foreign Generals (see note on *Praef.* 1, Atticus); it was he too who proposed that N. write a life of the elder Cato (see note on *Cato*. 3. 5, Atticus). And N. heard Atticus' funeral speech on his mother (*Att*. 17. 1). He tells us that he was a regular visitor at the *villa Tamphiliana* and claims 'familiaritas', 'acquaintance', with its owner Atticus (see note on 13. 7, This . . . relations). We shall see something both of how close and of how remote they were. Possibly, there is one neglected clue: informed treatment of Atticus' life in chronological sequence begins at 7. 1 (49 BC) and ends at 11. 4 (42 BC); certainly this was the most dangerous and eventful period of Atticus' life, but N. offers nothing else remotely comparable in terms of immediacy and detail, except for his account of Atticus' last illness. For the years after 42 there was no Cicero, and therefore there are no letters; we may suppose that Agrippa's father-in-law was suffered to pass his seventies in respected ease. N. had clearly seen something of his letters to Octavian (20. 2–3), but that does not prove necessarily N.'s close contact with Atticus in the 30s. Before 49 Cicero provides ample evidence for Atticus' involvement on the fringes of great events (SB i. 3 ff.); in N. there are only hints in passing. This particular emphasis may result in part from a conscious literary decision to focus above all on a short and specially significant period, but may also reflect the years of N.'s closest acquaintance.

But in its way, the *Atticus* is remarkable: 'this modest compiler essayed a startling novelty, for he included a *vita Attici*, when its subject was still among the living'.[1] N. recognized honestly, I suspect, the scale of his talents: obvious untruths (see notes on 14. 3, Mentana, income) and eager exaggerations (see notes on 9. 1, character, and 16. 3, letters) are infrequent and he records from a viewpoint if not intimate then clearly close enough at least for the

[1] R. Syme, *Sallust* (Berkeley 1964), 235.

biographer to learn something of the tone, language, and outlook of his subject (pp. 12–13). The detail is intermittently engrossing, if studied with care. N. had a fine nose, when he dared follow it. Repeatedly we wish for more of the same.

The flat, awkward prose of a man with no taste, or time, or capacity for elegance (cf. p. xviii) is in its way also telling: N. is uninventive, and his graceless language augments our sense of his essential honesty. The omissions, distortions, and overstatements are severally understandable and do limited damage. The reader is not called upon to reconsider any large-scale tendentious misinterpretation of his subject-matter (as he must do at times for Caesar, Sallust, Livy, and Tacitus among others). Paradoxically, this intermittently in-focus, rather monochrome, contemporary portrait of a major figure of the late republic has been blatantly neglected, even more by Latinists than by historians; lack of scholarly interest seems hard to justify and close study has greatly increased my respect for N. since my survey in 1982.

The life belongs to N.'s *Lives of the Latin Historians* (cf. the life of Cato above and frr. 56, 57, 58 below). It was not dedicated to Atticus,[2] as the consistent third-person narrative and description, the reference at *Cat.* 3. 5, and the occasional explicit uncertainties in N.'s mind (e.g. 4. 5, 19. 5) make clear. More important, perhaps, is the inclusion of Atticus' life in this volume in particular, which may suggest that this was how N. knew he wanted to be remembered and defined. Though N. says little (just chapter 18) of Atticus as scholar, what there is is vastly better than chapter 3 of the *Cato*.

Chapters 1–18 N. wrote in Atticus' lifetime, that is, before the end of March 32 BC; the reference to relations between Octavian and Antony (12. 1) suggests that N. cannot have been writing before 36/5.[3]

Chapters 19–22 (the appendix) belong between 32 and 27: Octavian is called 'Caesar' at 19. 3 and 'Octavian' at 20. 1, not 'Augustus', as he would have been after 27. Traces of additions elsewhere in the second edition have exercised scholars a good deal;[1] the 'I think' of 4. 5 just might have been inserted when N. realized he could no longer ask Atticus himself. It may, though, just as well be a detail from a period before N. and Atticus became acquainted, about which he preferred not to trouble his subject. It has also been suggested that the past tenses of chapters 13–18 could not have

[2] Cf. Geiger (1985), 99.
[3] Cf. Geiger (1985), 85, for example.
[4] Likewise the revision of the *Foreign Generals*. Summarised, Schanz–Hosius, 357; Geiger (1985), 85.

stood thus in Atticus' lifetime. That is not necessarily true;[5] we have no really parallel contemporary material and certainly no precedents. It may be that N. wrote thus even before 32 because the problem of describing the private life of a distinguished contemporary and social superior (but not immeasurably so) had not seriously been faced before; the perfect tenses, therefore, were perhaps an answer to a new social and stylistic problem. The appendix was added in haste: chapters 19–20 repeat a good deal of detail already used in 12. 1–2. N. apparently did not see fit to rework the earlier text.

I offer a schema of the life's structure: it is a good deal more complex and less clear-cut than those offered elsewhere.[6] There is a certain overlap between chapters 5 and 16–17; also between chapters 6 and 11. This has nothing to do with the problem of editions; N. is wrestling with the problem of how to organize his material both by chronological sequence and by topic without excessive duplication:

1	Family and education.
2–4	Athens. NB maintains contact with Rome (3. 4) and already shows 'humanitas' and 'doctrina' (4. 2).
5	Uncle Caecilius. Cicero and Q. Cicero. Q. Hortensius.
6	Begins *in re publica*, 'in public life': clearly a new subdivision starts here. Morality of public life; Atticus' non-participation.
7	7–9 all begin with a chronological indication; 7–11. 4 is arranged in chronological sequence.

7: 49–44
8–11. 4: 44–42
    11. 5–6 generalizes, reflects, exemplifies.
    12. 1–2
        3–5

13. 1 'No less good a head of a household than he was a citizen': clear sign that a major new section of the life starts here.

13: style of life: introduced by 'paterfamilias'; continued and developed in 14.
15: Att.'s character.
16: 'humanitas'.

[5] Stark (1964), 176, who points to the manner of a funeral poem written in the author's lifetime (Ov. *Trist.* 3. 3. 73–6).
[6] Cf. Leo (1901), 213 f.; Steidle (1951), 146.

17: 'pietas'.
18: love of antiquity and work as author.

19–22   Postscript added in second edition.

The place of the *Atticus* in the history of biography is complex and ambiguous. New it certainly is, but in just what way?—as the life of a living contemporary? It cannot be excluded that N.'s life of Cicero was also pre–43! Atticus is of course apolitical, yet a 'political animal' (see note on 8. 4, dissent); the life is in part a study of his avoidance of public life; that brings him close to being discussed as a type of negative political figure! He is placed, however, among the historians (see note on heading to the *Atticus*); a pair of books on usurers might have seemed tactless. Yet the historical activity takes up but a single chapter.

I summarize briefly some contributory literary elements: first, encomia, such as Xenophon's of Agesilaus and Isocrates' of Evagoras. Their relevance to the insistently laudatory tone of the *Atticus* has often been noted, and a possible verbal parallel exists with Xenophon's *Agesilaus*, which was very much read at Rome in N.'s day.[7] It is clearly also relevant to N.'s education as an author that writing the praises of famous men was an exercise in the schools of his youth.[8] Rhetoricians studied the 'classical' encomia that survived and evolved elaborate schemata for their structure; two are conveniently available.[9] The impartial reader is not struck by any overpoweringly obvious similarities.[10] It is equally clear that the very long tradition of funeral *laudationes* at Rome furthered the growth of biography, in some slightly remote and undefinable way.[11] Atticus *qua* scholar and historian might have suggested to N. analogies with the acknowledged Peripatetic interest in the lives of men of intellectual importance.[12] Autobiography too had become popular at Rome in the late republic;[13] Sulla was a notable practitioner.

---

[7] E. Jenkinson, *ANRW* i. 3. 708; Geiger (1985), 15 f.; Rawson (1985), 46, 62; N.'s possible echo: p. 12. See K. Münscher, *Philol.* suppl. 13/2 (1920), 75–82.

[8] Suet. *Rhet.* 1. 13; Cic. *de or.* 2. 341; Norden, *Antike Kunstprosa*, 204.

[9] Theon, *Rhet. Gr.* 2. 109 ff.; E. Jenkinson, *ANRW* i. 3. 796 ff., after Marrou (1956), 198 f.; Menander Rhetor, ed. N. G. Wilson and D. A. Russell (Oxford 1981), *Basilikos logos* (*Rhet. Gr.* 3. 368. 3 ff.), 77 ff.

[10] Cf. Leo (1901), 215.

[11] Cf. Rawson (1985), 229; Momigliano (1971), 94; see note on 17. 1 (mother's funeral); Atticus delivered one on his mother which N. heard.

[12] Momigliano (1971), 65 ff.; Geiger (1985), 51 ff.; M. Lefkowitz, *Lives of the Greek Poets* (London 1981).

[13] Momigliano (1971), 93 f.; Geiger (1985), 80; Rawson (1985), 227 ff.

It will be clear that we have no precise antecedent for the *Atticus*.
but a large number of approximate analogies. There is a danger that
an unrealistically close definition of what N.'s *Atticus* actually is can
be used artificially to enhance our perception of its author's
originality. 'Monographical works centred round the personality of
his patrons' is how Geiger describes what Voltacilius Pitholaus (if
that is his name) wrote about Pompeius Strabo and his son Magnus;
Momigliano says[14] 'biographies'.[14] Another example is Tiro on
Cicero, to whom we shall come shortly. Geiger is of course right to
say that surviving examples of the genre of historical monographs
concerned with the deeds of a single personality, such as Sallust's
Catiline and *Jugurtha*, are not at all the same thing as 'political
biography' (i.e. biography of political men).[15] So where is the
boundary drawn? Suetonius says that Voltacilius (?) wrote about
Pompey's 'res gestae', 'deeds', and that makes him an historian, but
Asconius refers to Tiro's fourth book on Cicero's life, *De vita eius*.[16]
The younger Cato, who died in 46, attracted memoirs contemporary
and posthumous, positive and negative; perhaps N. began his life of
the elder Cato in consequence.[17] N.'s *Cicero*, like Tiro's, is clearly
likelier than not to be post–43, though dates in Cicero's lifetime
cannot be excluded. N.'s novelty is not eliminated, but our
perception of his 'uniqueness' should have become a good deal
blurred.

N. writes of course both detailed biographies (of the elder Cato
and Cicero) and a very large biographical handbook (*De viris
illustribus*) as did Varro;[18] in Varro's *Imagines* the number of entries is
even larger (700 as against N.'s possible 400) and there were
pictures of each subject, but the individual entries were far slighter.
To the scale and structure of N.'s *De viris illustribus* scholars have
devoted a good deal of attention;[19] I summarize some conclusions.

There were perhaps as many as eighteen books and four hundred
lives; books were paired, with the foreigners in each category before
the Romans. Of categories identifiable, historians and generals are
certain; kings must go.[20] It is not clear to what group the *Letter of*

---

[14] Geiger (1985), 79; cf. Rawson (1985), 91 f., 229; on Voltacilius (?) it is N. himself
who is our source: see fr. 57 with note. Momigliano (1971), 95.
[15] Geiger (1985), 46 f., 9.
[16] Asconius, p. 48. 26 Clark; cf. Rawson (1985), 229: 'biography'.
[17] Cf. Geiger (1985), 100. The events of 44 attracted works about both Caesar and
Brutus (Rawson (1985), 229).
[18] Cf. Horsfall, *CHCL* ii. 843 f.; id., *CR* 28 (1978), 163.
[19] Geiger (1985), 84 ff. provides a useful updating.
[20] Geiger (1985), 87 f., 89 f.; id., *Lat.* 38 (1979), 662 ff.

Cornelia belongs.[21] The other categories have attracted a good deal of essentially inconclusive speculation.[22]

To several features of N.'s capacity as a biographer we must now turn in more detail than has hitherto been done: first, to his omissions: Atticus' publishing business has been said to be one of these.[23] Atticus did employ copyists (see note on 13. 3, copyists) but there is not a word in N. about a publishing business because it did not exist. More interesting, N. does not mention Epicureanism. Why not? Several patterns of explanation are possible (cf. note on 17. 3, philosophers). Odder, in a way, is the absence of Atticus' beloved (?second) wife Pilia (cf. note on 4. 3, head of a household). Her existence we infer only from references (e.g. 12. 1) to a daughter. Even Atticus' mother is concealed until 17. 1, and does not merit a mention with his father at 1. 2. Nothing in the life suggests that N. was an intimate of the whole family, as Cicero so clearly was; the ex-consul was partial to toddlers (cf. note on 12. 2, marriage). Perhaps a sense of tact or propriety on N.'s part reinforced the effects of ignorance or distance.

Secondly, for the period 44–2, N. offers a near-contemporary account. Though we may feel that the historical perspective is blurred, naïve, and overdramatized (cf. 8. 1; 8. 5; 9. 1), the language and outlook are not exceptional, and N. is trying tersely to set the life of a major, yet peripheral, figure coherently in the context of major developments. I have noted three significant occasions where N.'s account is without real parallel.[24] The first is a fleeting moment, barely glimpsed even in Cicero's letters and given undue emphasis by N.; neither of the other two is at all improbable or incredible (yes, one could imagine Cicero, old and angry, threatening death even to Antony's children!).

Thirdly, sources are seemingly never discussed in detail. I can only make some suggestions: from the Greek, 19. 1 may echo Xen. *Ages.* 10. 2, which N. is in any case likely (cf. p. 10) to have known. The clear echo of Plato at 22. 1 (cf. note, one . . . another) renders a passage already often turned by Cicero. N. had seen a collection of Cicero's letters to Atticus (16. 3)—pretty clearly not the collection that we now have—but there seems no definite indication that he used them.[25] But Cicero's *De amicitia*, for example, he knew very well, and much of what he says about Atticus' view of friendship,

[21] Cf. note on the letter (historians).

[22] Geiger (1985), 88 ff.; about Varro's *Imagines* we do know a little more!

[23] Stark (1964), 178 n. 4.

[24] 8. 1, the time when Brutus and Cassius were on top; 8. 3, the equestrian fund for Brutus and Cassius; 9. 2–3 the persecution of Antony's friends and family.

[25] Contrast J. Geiger, *Lat.* 44 (1985), 269 f.

central both to the life and to Epicurean ethics, is expressed in language that echoes closely Cicero's own treatise on friendship, dedicated to Atticus (cf. notes on 1. 4 (captivated) and 2. 1 (Sulpicius' brother), for example).

He was likewise familiar with Cicero's *De senectute* (see note on 4. 1, captured). And it was recently noted by Miriam Griffin, after C. Bailey, that though N. does not speak explicitly of Epicureanism, he repeatedly uses characteristically Epicurean language, which one must conclude that he had heard Atticus himself employ (cf. notes on 7. 3, inactivity, and 8. 4, scheme).[26] If that is a correct deduction, it shows not only that N. had listened with care to Atticus' discourse but had recorded significant details, though he pretty clearly had no intellectual sympathy (cf. note last cited). I have collected (see notes on 4. 2, lead me, and 17. 3, philosophers) a fair number of passages where N. explicitly reports a dictum or opinion of Atticus; given his very creditable echoing of Epicurean language, it is quite likely that several at least of these are authentic.

We may doubt whether Atticus appreciated either the modest stylistic abilities or the insistent didactic morality of his biographer. N.'s *naïveté* was forgivable with a smile, and his avoidance of gross factual error might even have been approved (cf. note on 14. 3 (income) for N. and the sources of Atticus' income). Positively, N. is notably receptive; he tries with some success to capture the spirit of the man and his age in significant detail and with apposite citation. Nothing, money-matters aside, rings clearly untrue. Much, in outlook and even at times in language, goes back to the subject himself. N. is disorganized, repetitive, schematic, priggish, yet Atticus must at times have acknowledged, however unwillingly, that he was recognizable as himself in those drably written pages.

It is hard to recommend further reading on N.'s *Atticus*. Momigliano (1971) mentions N. in passing; Geiger (1985) has many interesting observations set in complex professional polemic. My own discussion in *CHCL* ii was in part hasty and uninformed. Jenkinson's two treatments (*ANRW* i. 3. 704 ff. and in *Latin Biography*, ed. T. A. Dorey (London 1967), 1 ff.) overlap a good deal and do not illuminate much. No more do older books on biography in English: D. R. Stuart, *Epochs of Greek and Roman Biography* (Berkeley 1928, for example). Readers of German may consult O. Schönberger, *Das Altertum* 16 (1970), 153 ff., and R. Stark, *RhM* 107 (1964), 175 ff., and the treatments in Leo (1901), 213 ff. and Steidle (1951), 146 ff. Note further some helpful observations in V. d'Agostino, *Riv. stud. class.* 10 (1962), 109 ff., and J. André and A.

---

[26] M. Griffin, *G & R* 33 (1986), 76 n. 6.

Hus, *L'Histoire à Rome* (Paris 1974), 57 ff. But the only discussion of N. known to me that radiates real intellectual energy and distinction is that by E. Norden on his style (cf. p. xviii). Of earlier editions, Nipperdey–Witte (often reprinted; I have used the eleventh edition, Berlin 1913) proved far more helpful than that of M. Ruch (Paris 1968). On Atticus the man, we are far better served: see SB i. 3 ff.; Byrne (1920); Drumann v². 8 ff.; R. Feger in Pauly–Wissowa, Suppl. 8 (1956), 503 ff.; R. J. Leslie, *The Epicureanism of T. Pomponius Atticus* (Philadelphia 1950), with the review by C. Bailey, *JRS* 41 (1951), 163 f.

From the Book of Cornelius Nepos,
'On the Latin Historians'; life of Atticus

(**1. 1**) Titus Pomponius Atticus, descended as he was from the remotest origins of the Roman race, retained uninterrupted the equestrian rank inherited from his forbears. (**1. 2**) His father was industrious, by the standards of those days rich, and a lover of literature. He, in keeping with his love of letters, instructed his son in all those branches of learning in which boyhood should be made to share. (**1. 3**) As a boy, in addition to a natural aptitude for learning, he had also an exceptional charm of expression and tone, so he not only took in swiftly what was communicated, but also recited it extremely well. In consequence he had a notable reputation among his contemporaries and shone forth more brightly than his noble-spirited friends could bear with equanimity. (**1. 4**) So he roused them all by his own enthusiasm: among their number were Lucius Torquatus, Gaius Marius (the son), and Marcus Cicero. He so captivated them all by his company that no one was dearer to them for all their lives.

(**2. 1**) His father died early. As a young man, on account of a family connection with Publius Sulpicius, who was killed when tribune of the people, he had some share in that danger; for Anicia, a cousin of Pomponius on his mother's side, had married Servius, Sulpicius' brother. (**2. 2**) So when Sulpicius was killed and Atticus saw that the state was thrown into turmoil by the disorder Cinna provoked, and that he was vouchsafed no opportunity to live in keeping with his standing without offending one side or the other—the Romans' loyalties were divided and some favoured the cause of Sulla, others that of Cinna—he thought the time was right to devote himself to his studies and moved to Athens. Nonetheless he helped the young Marius from his own resources when he had been adjudged an enemy of that state and relieved his flight with financial help. (**2. 3**) And so that his time abroad should do his estate no harm, he moved a large part of his fortune to Athens. Here he lived in such a manner that he became greatly beloved of all the Athenians, for good reason. (**2. 4**) For apart from the charm which was already abundant when he was a young man, he often relieved their public want from his own resources: when they were obliged to raise a public loan and were unable to obtain fair terms for it, he always stepped in, on terms: he never accepted interest from them nor allowed them to continue the loan beyond the term fixed. (**2. 5**) Both conditions were good for the Athenians: he neither suffered their debt to become established through his leniency nor to grow through the multiplication of the interest. (**2. 6**) He augmented this service by a further generous action: he gave them all corn on a scale of six pecks of wheat per head: this measure is called a medimnus at Athens.

(**3. 1**) At Athens he so behaved as to seem at one with the humblest and on a level with the mighty. The result was that they bestowed on him all the public honours possible and sought to make him a citizen. Of this kind offer he was unwilling to take advantage. (**3. 2**) As long as he lived there, he took a stand against the erection of any statue to him, but when absent he could not stop them. So they put up several statues to him in their most hallowed places, for in all the management of the state's business, they treated him as both agent and counsel. (**3. 3**) It was, therefore, fortune's chief gift that he was born in that very city where dwelt rule over the world, so that it was for him both native land and home; on the other hand, it was a sign of his wisdom that when he moved to the city which excelled all others in its antiquity, its culture, and its learning, he was uniquely dear to it.

(**4. 1**) When Sulla, on his way back from Asia, came to Athens, he kept Pomponius by him as long as he was there, captured by the young man's qualities of culture and learning. He spoke Greek so well that he seemed a native Athenian; so agreeable was his Latin that its charm seemed somehow inborn, not acquired. He also delivered poetry, both in Greek and in Latin, so well that there was nothing further to be added. (**4. 2**) So it happened that Sulla at no point let him go

and wanted to take him back with him to Italy. When Sulla
tried to convince him, 'No, please, I beg you,' said Atticus, 'I
left Italy to avoid bearing arms against you in the company of
those men against whom you would lead me.' Sulla commended
the young man's sense of duty, and ordered all the presents
which he had received at Athens to be passed on to him at his
departure. (**4. 3**) He stayed at Athens for several years: he
gave as much attention to his family estate as the conscientious
head of a household should, and devoted all the rest of his
time either to literature or to the Athenians' public affairs;
nevertheless he placed himself at the service of his friends in
Rome for he went regularly to their elections (**4. 4**) and if
anything of major importance arose did not fail them; thus, he
was exceptionally loyal to Cicero in all his perils: when he fled
his country, Atticus made him a present of 250,000 sesterces.
(**4. 5**) When affairs at Rome were restored to calm, he
returned, I think when Lucius Cotta and Lucius Torquatus
were consuls: on his departure the whole citizen body of
Athens escorted him and by their tears indicated their grief at
his coming absence.

(**5. 1**) He had an uncle, Quintus Caecilius, a Roman knight
and a friend of Lucius Lucullus, a rich man and of a very
difficult character: Atticus so respected his acerbity that he
gave no offence and retained his goodwill—no one else could
stand him—down to his old age and thereby reaped the fruits
of his devotion, (**5. 2**) for Caecilius at his death adopted him
in his will and made him heir to three-quarters of his estate:
from this inheritance he received about 10 million sesterces.
(**5. 3**) Atticus' sister was married to Quintus Tullius Cicero,
and Marcus Cicero had arranged this match; with Marcus,
Atticus lived on very close terms since they were pupils
together, much more intimately indeed than with Quintus, so
it may be concluded that similarity of character carries more
weight in friendship than ties of blood. (**5. 4**) He was also on
such intimate terms with Quintus Hortensius, who was the
leading orator of the day, that one could not decide whether
Cicero or Hortensius loved him more dearly, and he achieved
the very difficult feat that there was no rancour between two

men who so competed for renown; he was himself the bond
between two such distinguished men.

(**6. 1**) His conduct in public life was such that he always
belonged and was recognized as belonging to the *optimates*; yet
he did not commit himself to the storms of civil disorder, for
he considered that men who entrusted themselves to such
waves were no more in control than those who were tossed by
the waves of the sea. (**6. 2**) He sought no offices, though they
lay open to him through both his influence and his standing:
neither could they be sought in the traditional manner, nor
could they be won without breaking the law amid the bribery
such unrestrained canvassing involved, nor could they be held
to the state's advantage without danger when public morals
had been so corrupted. (**6. 3**) He never took part in a public
auction; for no enterprise did he become a surety or a
contractor; he accused no one, whether in his own name or as
seconder; he never went to law on his own account; he never
exercised jurisdiction. (**6. 4**) The post of prefect, offered him
by many consuls and praetors he accepted on condition that
he accompany no one to his province, be content with the
honour alone, and despise the profit to his estate; not even
with Quintus Cicero had he wanted to go to Asia, though he
had the chance of a legate's position on his staff, for he said
that it was not seemly, when he had refused to hold a
praetorship, to be a praetor's assistant. (**6. 5**) He served
therein the interests not only of his dignity but also of his ease,
since he avoided any suspicions of crime. His regard was
consequently valued by everyone, since they realized it was to
be attributed neither to fear nor to hope, but to his sense of
duty.

(**7. 1**) When he was about 60, there occurred Caesar's civil
war. He took advantage of the exemption conferred by his age,
and did not move away from Rome. From his own fortune he
gave everything that his friends had needed as they set off to
Pompey; Pompey himself, close though he was to him, he did
not offend. (**7. 2**) From him he was holding no mark of
distinction, as others did, who had received either office or
money through him; some of them most reluctantly followed

his army, part remained at Rome and gave him the greatest offence. (**7. 3**) Atticus' inactivity was so welcome to Caesar that when he had won and was requesting money from private individuals by letter, not only did he give Atticus no trouble, but pardoned at his request his sister's son and Quintus Cicero, in Pompey's camp as they were. Thus he escaped new dangers by his old rule of life.

(**8. 1**) After Caesar's death, when it seemed that the state was in the hands of the two Brutuses and Cassius, and that all the citizens had turned to them, (**8. 2**) he was on such good terms with Marcus Brutus that the young man was not closer to any of his contemporaries than he was to Atticus, old though he was. Brutus kept him not only as a leading adviser, but also as a daily companion. (**8. 3**) Some people devised the idea that a private fund should be set up for Caesar's assassins by the Roman knights. They thought it could easily be brought about if the leading men of the order contributed money. So Atticus was appealed to by Gaius Flavius, an intimate of Brutus, to lead the scheme. (**8. 4**) But because he thought that services should be performed for friends without taking sides, and had always kept away from that sort of plan, he replied that if Brutus wished to make any use of his resources he might do so as far as they permitted, but that he would neither discuss nor join with anyone in that scheme. So the conspiratorial association was shattered just by this one man's dissent. (**8. 5**) Not long after, Antony began to get on top, so Brutus and Cassius abandoned their attention to the duties assigned to them by the consul for the sake of appearances, despaired of the situation, and went into exile. (**8. 6**) Atticus, who had refused to contribute money, along with others, to that cause when it was prospering, sent Brutus as a present 100,000 sesterces when he was in desperate straits and leaving Italy. In his absence, he gave orders for another 300,000 to be given to Brutus in Epirus. Antony he flattered no more in his time of power; no more did he abandon those in despair.

(**9. 1**) There followed the war fought at Modena: during it, if I just called him sensible, I should commend him less than I should, since he was more a seer, if by the character of a seer we mean an enduring inborn goodness which no vicissitudes unsettle or lessen. (**9. 2**) Antony was adjudged a public enemy and left Italy. There was no hope of his restoration. Not only his enemies, who were at that time very powerful and numerous, but also those who had sided with his opponents and hoped by doing him harm to gain some advantage, began to attack Antony's friends, wanted to strip his wife Fulvia of all her possessions and even sought to put his children to death. (**9. 3**) Atticus, though he was a very close intimate of Cicero, and a dear friend of Brutus, not only gave them no encouragement towards outraging Antony, but on the contrary protected, as far as he could, those close to him as they fled from Rome, and helped them with what they were short of: (**9. 4**) on Publius Volumnius he bestowed so much that more could not have come from a parent. To Fulvia herself when she was distracted by lawsuits and tormented by great fears, so assiduously did he perform his services that she never kept bail without Atticus, and Atticus was in all matters her surety. (**9. 5**) He even, since she had in the days of her good fortune bought an estate, to be paid for by a fixed date, and was unable, after the catastrophe, to raise a loan, stepped in and entrusted her with the money, with no interest and on no formal terms, thinking it his greatest gain to be acknowledged as mindful of and grateful for favours, and at the same time to make it plain that he was accustomed to be a friend not to success, but to people. (**9. 6**) No one could think that he acted thus under force of circumstances, for no one believed that Antony would triumph. (**9. 7**) But he was most fiercely criticized by several *optimates* because they thought he seemed insufficiently to hate 'bad' citizens. Atticus, however, relied on his own judgement and considered what it was right for him to do rather than what others were going to commend.

(**10. 1**) Fortune suddenly turned. When Antony came back to Italy, everyone had thought that Atticus would be in great danger because of his very close friendship with Cicero and Brutus, (**10. 2**) so just before the general's homecoming he had withdrawn from public life and was in hiding at Publius Volumnius', whom, as I have explained, he had helped shortly before. Such was the changeability of fortune at that time that now one side, now the other was at the extremes either of success or of danger; he had with him Quintus Gellius Canus, a contemporary and a man very like him. (**10. 3**) This may also serve as an instance of Atticus' goodness that he lived on such close terms with Canus, whom he had known as a boy at school, that their friendship grew down to their old age. (**10. 4**) But Antony, even though he was spurred on by such hatred for Cicero that he was an enemy not only to him but to all his friends and wanted to proscribe them, as many encouraged him to do, still remembered Atticus' services and after he had found out where he was, wrote to him in his own hand telling him not to be afraid and to come to him at once; he had removed him, and for his sake Canus, from the list of the proscribed. (**10. 5**) And so he should run no danger—that used to occur at night—he sent him a guard. So Atticus at a time of great danger served to protect not only himself but also the friend whom he held dearest. Nor did he seek assistance from anyone for his own security in isolation, but did so also for his friend's, so that it appeared that he wished for no good fortune for himself alone, independently of Canus. (**10. 6**) But if the helmsman who saves the ship from a storm in a reef-filled sea is exalted with particular praise, why should not the foresight of a man who reached safety after such grave and numerous squalls of civil strife be thought remarkable?

(**11. 1**) After he emerged from these troubles, he devoted all his attentions to helping as many people as he could and in whatever ways. When the mob was seeking out those proscribed for the rewards offered by the generals, there was no one who came to Epirus who lacked for anything and everyone was granted the means to stay there for good. (**11. 2**) After the battle at Philippi and the death of Gaius Cassius and Marcus Brutus, he even began to protect Lucius Iulius Mocilla, the ex-praetor, and his son, and Aulus Torquatus, and those others struck down by a like blow of fortune, and gave orders that all their needs should be transported from Epirus to Samothrace. It is hard to cover all the details, nor is it necessary. (**11. 3**) I want one point to be understood, that his generosity did not depend on circumstances or on calculation. (**11. 4**) It may be concluded from the facts and circumstances themselves that he did not sell himself to the successful but always helped those in trouble. He even took care of Servilia, Brutus' mother, no less after his death than while she prospered. (**11. 5**) He was magnanimous and pursued no feuds, since he harmed no one, and if he had received some injury, certainly preferred to forget, not to avenge. He likewise retained the kindnesses he had received in an unfading memory, while those he had himself bestowed he remembered for as long as the recipient was grateful. (**11. 6**) He so acted as to bear out the truth of the saying 'each man's character moulds his own fortune'. Nor did he mould his fortune before he moulded himself, and took care not to be blamed with justification in any matter.

(**12. 1**) So by these means he brought it about that Marcus Vipsanius Agrippa, who was linked to the young Caesar by the closest friendship, though on account of his own influence and Caesar's power he had the opportunity of any match, chose a relationship by marriage with Atticus in particular, and preferred the daughter of a Roman knight to wedlock with an aristocratic bride. (**12. 2**) It was—and this is not to be concealed—Marcus Antonius, triumvir for re-establishing the republic, who brought about this marriage. When Atticus might have increased his properties through Agrippa's influence, so far was he from a lust for money that he only used that influence in begging the removal of his friends' dangers or inconveniences. (**12. 3**) This was really quite remarkable during the proscription itself, for when the triumvirs, after the practice under which things were done at the time, sold the property of Lucius Saufeius, a Roman knight and a contemporary of Atticus, who was drawn by his love of philosophy to live several years in Athens, but held valuable estates in Italy, Atticus' good work and efforts brought it about that it was by the same messenger that Saufeius was informed both that he had lost, and that he had regained, his inheritance. (**12. 4**) He likewise rescued Lucius Julius Calidus, who I truly think I can maintain is much the most elegant poet which our age has produced after the death of Lucretius and Catullus, and no less a good man and well educated in the most important branches of knowledge, who was in his absence entered in the register of the proscribed by Publius Volumnius, Antony's aide-de-camp, after the proscription of the knights, on account of his large properties in Africa. (**12. 5**) It is hard to determine whether it was at the time more toilsome or more glorious for Atticus, since it was recognized that in their time of peril he cared for his friends both present and absent.

(**13. 1**) But he was regarded as no less good a head of a household than he was a citizen. For though he was wealthy, no man was less partial to buying and to building. However, he did live extremely well and everything he used was of the best. (**13. 2**) For his house, once Tamphilus', was on the Quirinal hill; it had been bequeathed to him by his uncle, and its charm lay not in the building but in the grounds, for the structure itself was built long ago and had more character than luxury. In it he changed nothing except in cases when he was forced to by its age. (**13. 3**) His slave household, to judge by its practical qualities, was outstanding; to judge by its beauty, barely adequate. For among it there were highly-educated slaves, excellent readers, and numerous copyists, so there was not even a single footman who could not both read and copy finely. Likewise, the other specialists required by domestic comfort were particularly good. (**13. 4**) Every one of them was born and trained in the household; this is a sign not only of his restraint but also of his industry, for, first, not to have immoderate desires, such as you would very frequently see, should be thought the sign of a self-restrained man, and, second, to procure by effort rather than by outlay is a sign of considerable determination. (**13. 5**) He was of good taste, not lordly, splendid not lavish, and with all his efforts aimed not at affluence but at elegance. His furnishings were moderate not copious, to be noted for neither excess. (**13. 6**) Nor shall I omit, though I think some may judge it trivial, that though he was an exceptionally substantial Roman knight and invited to his home very generously men of all ranks, he used to allow 3,000 sesterces a month on average for domestic expenses from his accounts. (**13. 7**) This I assert as a matter not reported but observed, for I often joined in his life at home on account of our relations.

(**14. 1**) At dinner no one heard any entertainment other than a reader (quite delightful, I think), nor was there ever a dinner at his house without some reading to please his guests' minds not less than their bellies; (**14. 2**) for he used to invite people whose way of life was not incompatible with his own. When the great increase in his wealth occurred, he changed nothing of his daily style of life and displayed such moderation that neither on the 2 m. sesterces which he had inherited from his father did he live with insufficient splendour, nor on 10 m. did he live in greater affluence than to begin with, and on both fortunes stayed on the same level. (**14. 3**) He had no park, no luxurious villa near Rome or by the sea, nor any country estate in Italy, but for those at Arezzo and Mentana. All his financial income consisted of properties in Epirus and Rome from which one can tell that he used to measure the value of money not by quantity but by reason.

(**15. 1**) Lies he never told nor could he endure. So his courtesy did not lack severity nor his gravity charm, so it was hard to understand whether his friends more respected or loved him. If a request was made him, he gave his word scrupulously, because he thought it irresponsibility not generosity to promise what he could not perform. (**15. 2**) He was likewise so careful in attending to things once he had promised them that he gave the impression of carrying out not a commission but his own business. Never did he tire of a business once undertaken: for he thought his own reputation was involved therein, and than that there was nothing dearer to him. (**15. 3**) So the result was that he looked after all the business affairs of the Ciceros, of Marcus Cato, Quintus Hortensius, Aulus Torquatus, and of many Roman knights besides. So the judgement is permissible that he avoided administration of the state's business not from idleness but from choice.

(**16. 1**) No greater proof of his humanity can I produce than that as a young man he was most dear to Sulla in his old age, yet likewise as an old man was the same to the young Marcus Brutus, while with his contemporaries Quintus Hortensius and Marcus Cicero he lived on such good terms that it is hard to judge to which generation he was best suited. (**16. 2**)

Nevertheless Cicero was particularly fond of him: so much so that not even his own brother Quintus was dearer or closer. (**16. 3**) To prove the point, apart from the books in which Cicero mentions Atticus, which have been published, there are eleven rolls of letters, sent to Atticus from the time of Cicero's consulship right down to the end: the reader would little need a continuous history of the period. (**16. 4**) For they offer so full a record of everything to do with statesmens' policies, generals' failings, and changes in the state that nothing does not appear in them and it is easy to think that Cicero's good sense was in some way prophetic, for not only did he predict things which happened in his lifetime, but also sang like a prophet of matters now in current use.

(**17. 1**) What more should I relate of Atticus' devotion to his family? I heard him really boasting of just this at his mother's funeral, whom he buried at the age of ninety, when he was himself sixty-seven, that he was never reconciled with his mother nor quarrelled with his sister, who was roughly his contemporary. (**17. 2**) That is a sign either that no dispute had ever occurred between them or that he was so indulgent towards his family that he judged it wicked to be angry with those whom he ought to love. (**17. 3**) Nor did he do this because of nature alone, though we all obey her but also on account of his reading, for he had so fully perceived the precepts of the leading philosophers that he employed them for conducting his life, not for show.

(**18. 1**) He was a leading follower of ancestral custom and lover of antiquity, which he had so thoroughly mastered, that he set it all out in the volume in which he placed the magistracies in order. (**18. 2**) For there is no law or treaty nor important event in Roman history which is not recorded therein under its date and—this was very difficult—he so worked on the origin of families that from it we can learn the offspring of famous men. (**18. 3**) He did the same thing for individual families in his other books: thus at the request of Marcus Brutus he enumerated the Junian family from its origin to the present, recording who was whose son, what magistracies he held, and when. (**18. 4**) He did the same at

Claudius Marcellus' request on the Marcelli, at Cornelius Scipio's and Fabius Maximus' on the Fabii and Aemilii. Nothing can be more delightful than these books to those who have some desire for knowledge about famous men. (**18. 5**) He also touched on poetry so as to have some part, I suppose, in its charm, for it was in verse that he so held forth on those who surpassed the rest of the Roman people in honours received and in the grandeur of their deeds that (**18. 6**) beneath the portraits of each of them he described their deeds and magistracies in not more than four or five lines at a time. It is barely credible that such great achievements could be set forth so concisely. There is also a single roll written in Greek on the consulate of Cicero.

(**19. 1**) This much I published in Atticus' lifetime. Now, since fortune has willed that I survive him, I shall cover the remainder and so far as possible instruct my readers by means of actual examples, as I indicated above that for the most part it is each man's character that secures his fortune. (**19. 2**) For happy as he was with the equestrian rank in which he was born, he entered the family of the emperor, son of the deified Caesar; he had already reached terms of friendship previously, exclusively by means of the elegant style of life thanks to which he had captivated the other leading men in the state, Octavian's equals in standing but inferiors in good fortune. (**19. 3**) For such success befell Caesar that Fortune bestowed on him everything that she had bestowed on anyone previously and won him what no Roman citizen was able to achieve hitherto. (**19. 4**) To Atticus there was born a granddaughter, the child of Agrippa to whom he had given his daughter in marriage as a girl. This granddaughter Caesar betrothed when she was scarcely a year old to Tiberius Claudius Nero his stepson, the son of Drusilla. This link confirmed their close relations and rendered their friendly intercourse more frequent.

(**20. 1**) Still, even before this betrothal, when Octavian was away from Rome, he never sent a letter to any friend or kinsman without word to Atticus on what he was doing and above all on what he was reading, and where and for how long he was going to be staying. (**20. 2**) But also, when he was in

Rome and enjoyed Atticus' company less often than he might wish on account of his innumerable activities, hardly a single day passed on which he did not write to him: sometimes he asked him something about antiquity, sometimes he put him some problem in poetry, at times he jestingly coaxed longer letters from him. (**20. 3**) So it happened that when the temple of Jupiter Feretrius on the Capitol, founded by Romulus, had lost its roof from age and neglect and was collapsing, it was at Atticus' urging that Caesar saw to its restoration. (**20. 4**) On the other hand Marcus Antonius cultivated him in correspondence no less, when at a distance, and so took care to inform Atticus exactly on what he was doing from far-distant lands. (**20. 5**) Just what this means will be more readily appreciated by a reader who can judge what a sign of wisdom it was to retain the society and goodwill of those two men between whom there intervened not only a competition for the highest prizes, but such an exchange of insults as was bound to occur between Caesar and Antony when each of them desired to be the leading man not only of the city of Rome but of the world.

(**21. 1**) When he had completed seventy-seven years in such a manner, and into extreme old age had advanced no less in dignity than in influence and riches (for he obtained many inheritances exclusively by his own goodness), and had enjoyed such good health that he had not needed medicine for thirty years, he fell ill: (**21. 2**) to begin with neither he nor the doctors took it seriously, for they thought it was a griping of the bowel for which swift and simple remedies were proposed. (**21. 3**) When he had passed three months in this condition without any pains but for those he experienced from the treatment, the disease burst so violently into his lower intestine that at the end ulcers full of matter burst through his loins. (**21. 4**) And before this befell him, after he felt the pains increase daily and the fever grow, he gave instructions for his son-in-law Agrippa to be summoned, and Lucius Cornelius Balbus and Sextus Peducaeus along with him. (**21. 5**) When he saw they had come, he leaned on one elbow and said: 'Just how much care and attention I have employed in caring for my health recently I do not need to recount at length, since I have you as witnesses. Since I have, I hope, satisfied you that I have left undone nothing that might serve to cure me, all that is left is that I now look after my own interests. This I wished you to know: for I am resolved no longer to nourish the disease. (**21. 6**) For however much food I have taken in these last days, I have so prolonged my life as to increase the pain without hope of recovery. So I beg of you both to approve of my plan and not to try to hinder me by pointless dissuasion.'

(**22. 1**) After delivering this speech with such resolve in his voice and expression that he seemed to be moving not from life but from one house to another, (**22. 2**) Agrippa in particular embraced him in tears and begged him not to hasten his death over and above nature's compulsion, and, since even then he might survive the crisis, to preserve himself for himself and for those dearest to him, but Atticus quelled his pleas with silent obstinacy. (**22. 3**) So when he had abstained from food for two days, the fever suddenly ceased and the illness began to be more bearable. Nevertheless he carried through his intention undeviatingly and so died, on the fifth day after he formed the plan, on the last day of March when Cnaeus Domitius and Gaius Sosius were consuls. (**22. 4**) He was carried to burial on a modest bier as he had himself directed, without any funeral procession, but escorted by all men of substance and by very large crowds of the common people. He was buried by the Appian Way at the fifth milestone, in the tomb of Quintus Caecilius his uncle.

PROLOGUE TO THE LIVES OF THE FOREIGN GENERALS

Cornelius Nepos, 'Book of the Leading Generals of Foreign Nations';
Prologue

(**1**) I am sure, Atticus, that there will be a great many people who judge this kind of writing frivolous and insufficiently worthy of the characters of great men, when they read a report of who taught Epaminondas music, or find it mentioned among his virtues that he danced gracefully and played skilfully on the pipes. (**2**) They will in general be those who, ignorant of Greek literature, think nothing right unless it squares with their own morality. (**3**) But if they discover that not everyone has the same view of what is proper, and what disgraceful conduct, but that everything is judged by ancestral practice, they will not be surprised that in recounting the Greeks' virtues, I have followed their standards. (**4**) For it was no disgrace for Cimon, a leading Athenian, to marry his half-sister, since his fellow citizens followed the same practice. But it is really regarded as an outrage by our moral standards. In Crete it is regarded as praiseworthy for youths to have as many lovers as possible. There is no Spartan widow of such high birth that she will not go to a dinner party hired for a fee. (**5**) In almost all of Greece, it was among matters for high praise to be proclaimed a victor at Olympia; to appear on the stage and to be viewed by the populace, no one regarded as a matter for disgrace, among those same nations. At Rome all these acts are regarded as, in part, dishonouring, in part, low and alien to decent behaviour. (**6**) On the other hand, there are numerous actions decent by our standards which are thought base by them. For what Roman is ashamed to take his wife to a dinner party? Where does the lady of the house not occupy the place of honour, and receive guests? This is all very different in Greece: (**7**) she is only invited to dinners of the family and sits only in the inner part of the house, which is called the women's quarters: no one enters unless bound by ties of kinship. (**8**) but both the scale of the volume and my haste to unfold what I have begun prevent me from giving over more instances here. So let me come to the point and in this book give an account of the lives of the leading generals.

NEPOS: SELECTED FRAGMENTS

The fragments are numbered after Marshall, 101 ff.

Chronica

2. Catul. 1. 1–7

To whom do I give my charming, new, little book, just
brought to a shine with dry pumice? Cornelius, to you. For
you used to think my trifles really were something, even then,
when you were the only one of the Italians to venture to unfold
all history in three volumes, learned ones, by Jupiter, and full
of hard work.

4. Gell. 17. 21. 3

For with regard to Homer and Hesiod, almost all writers
agree that either they lived at about the same time or that
Homer was somewhat the earlier but that both lived before
the foundation of Rome, while the Silvii ruled at Alba, more
than 160 years after the Trojan war, as Cassius [Hemina] has
recorded in the first book of his *Annales* about Homer and
Hesiod, but as Cornelius Nepos said in the first book of his
Chronica about Homer, about 160 years before the foundation
of Rome.

5. See below; cited in commentary on fragment 9.

6. Gell. 15. 16. 1

Milo of Croton, the famous athlete who is said in the
chronicles to have been crowned for the first time in the [sixty-
second] Olympiad [= 532 BC] had a sad and wonderful
departure from this life.

7. Gell. 17. 21. 8

Cornelius Nepos says that while Tullus Hostilius was reigning
at Rome, Archilochus was even then famed and well known
for his poems.

8. Gell. 17. 21. 23

Not much later Marcus Manlius, who had driven back downhill the Gauls creeping up the steep way during the siege of the Capitol, was convicted at Rome of having formed a plan to seize absolute power; he was condemned to death, and thrown, according to Varro, from the Tarpeian rock, but as Cornelius Nepos left on record, was flogged to death.

9. Solin. 40. 4

So it is recorded that the temple at Ephesus burned down the same day as Alexander the Great was born at Pella: as Nepos declares, he was born when Marcus Fabius Ambustus and Titus Quintius Capitolinus were consuls in the three hundred and eighty-fifth year after the foundation of Rome.

37. From the *Life of Cicero*, Gell. 15. 28. 1 f.

Cornelius Nepos was a most particular student of records and a specially close friend of Cicero. But in the first book of his *Life of Cicero* he seems to have erred in writing that he [Cicero] pleaded hs first case and defended Sextus Roscius, accused of parricide, at the age of 23.

38. Hieron. *Contra Ioann. Ierosol.* 12 (*PL* xxiii. 381)

For Cornelius Nepos reports that, in his presence, Cicero pleaded the defence of Cornelius, the seditious tribune in nearly the same words in which it was published.

Letters

39. Lac. *Div. inst.* 3. 15. 10

Cornelius Nepos also writes to Cicero as follows: 'So far am I from thinking that philosophy is the mistress of life and the means to achieving happiness that I believe that none need masters in their lives more than most of those who occupy themselves with discussing philosophy. For I observe that most of those who lay down the law about modesty and continence so cleverly in the schools live amid all the desires and passions.

De viris illustribus

54. Suet. *Poet*. 6. 3

Nepos says that he found, from a reliable source, that Gaius
Laelius once, in his villa at Puteoli, on the kalends of March,
was bidden to come to dinner early by his wife and asked her
not to interrupt. When he finally entered the dining room,
late, he said that things had not often turned out better in his
writing. He was then asked to read out what he had written
and recited these verses in the *Self-Tormentor*: 'Syrus' promises
have brought me here, cheekily enough, by Pollux' [723].

56. Gell. 11. 8

Marcus Cato is said to have reproved Aulus Albinus in a
particularly appropriate and delightful way. Albinus, who
was consul with Lucius Lucullus [151 BC] used to write on
Roman history in Greek. At the beginning of his History, he
writes in these terms: it was not appropriate for anyone to be
angry with him if there was anything in his volume that was
written in a rather disorderly or not very elegant way. 'For I
am', he said, 'a Roman born in Latium; Greek is altogether
foreign to me.' So he requested pardon and understanding for
any unfavourable judgement for such flaws as there were.
When Marcus Cato read this, he said, 'Aulus, you really are a
proper ass: you prefer to deprecate blame rather than not to
attract it. I ask pardon for error without thought or for faults
under constraint. Who drove you, might I ask, to do
something for which you asked for forgiveness before you did
it?'

57. Suet. *Rhet*. 3

[L. Voltacilius Pitholaus] taught Cn. Pompeius Magnus and
recounted both his father's achievements and his in several
books; he was the first freedman, according to Cornelius
Nepos, to attempt to write history, which had until then been
the exclusive preserve of men of very good family.

58. An excerpt from the *De historicis latinis*, in praise of Cicero,
apparently found in 1759 in Cod. Guelf. Gud. lat. 278.

You should realize that this is one branch of Latin literature which not only does not rise to the level of Greece but was left really rough and sketchy by the death of Cicero. For he was the one man who could, and also should, have expressed our history in the language it deserved, since he was the man who inherited oratorical eloquence in its rough state from our ancestors and polished it thoroughly; philosophy in Latin, which was previously uncouth, he moulded in his own language. In consequence I am uncertain whether Rome or History grieves more at his death. . . .

61. Suet. *Gram.* 3

The term 'grammarians' [grammatici], after the Greek manner, prevailed, but initially they were called 'men of letters' [litterati]. Cornelius Nepos too, in the pamphlet in which he distinguishes the man of letters [litteratus] from the scholar [eruditus], says that at least in common parlance 'man of letters' is used of those able to speak or write with care, clarity, and knowledge, but strictly that is how the interpreters of poetry ought to be described; by the Greeks they are called grammarians.

62. Suet. *Aug.* 77

Octavian was also most frugal by nature in his consumption of wine. Nepos relates that encamped before Modena he drank not more than three cups.

CATO: SELECTED FRAGMENTS

Speeches

There are well over two hundred fragments from over eighty speeches. Two modern editions exist: E. Malcovati, *ORF²* (Turin 1955), 12 ff., and M. T. Sblendorio Cugusi, *Marci Porci Catonis orationum reliquiae* (Turin 1982). Modern discussions are abundant: Astin (1978), 131 ff.; Kennedy (1972), 38 ff.; M. L. Clarke, *Rhetoric at Rome* (London 1953), 39 ff.; Gratwick, *CHCL* ii 152 ff. We are also generously provided with ancient assessments of Cato as an orator; compare Astin (1978), 139 ff. with (for example) Cic. *Brut.* 63–9, Tac. *Dial.* 18, Plut. *Cat. mai.* 7, Liv. 39. 40. 7 f. But nothing matches the fragments themselves to give the flavour of the man and of his brutal, witty eloquence: some are translated in the modern discussions cited; very many others are to be found in the Loeb edition of Aulus Gellius (index s.v. Porcius Cato, Censorius, M., *orationes*). This was the man who said 'stick to the point; the words will follow' and who defined an orator as 'a good man experienced in speaking' (*To his son on rhetoric*, frr. 14, 15 Jordan). Compare his remarks on what happened when Greek interpreters tried to translate him (Plut. *Cat. mai.* 12. 5).

Origines

The fragments are numbered after *HRR* i. 51 ff.; I give in parentheses the source of the fragment only when it is reasonably accessible.

1.

If there are any men whom it pleases to describe the achievements of the Roman people . . .

2. (= Cic. *Planc.* 66)

Men in the public view and distinguished should be able to account for their leisure as well as for their official activities . . .

3. Either we commend the advantage of history in general as does Cato . . .

Frr. **4–13** on the Aeneas legend bristle with problems; for a brief guide with ample bibliography see Bremmer and Horsfall (1987), 12 ff.

17. D. H. 1. 74. 2

Porcius Cato does not give a Greek definition of time but is, if anyone, careful with regard to gathering material for Rome's early history, and says that the foundation of Rome came 432 years after the fall of Troy.

21. Antemna is even older than Rome.

31. Serv. ad Verg. *Aen.* 11. 715

. . . but as to where they [the Ligurians] are from, all memory has perished; they are illiterate and liars and have little recollection of the truth.

51. Serv. ad Verg. *Aen.* 8. 638

But Cato and Gellius say that they [the Sabines] are descended from Sabus the Lacedaemonian. Every text confirms that the Spartans were extremely hardy and Cato likewise says that the Roman people followed the Sabines' mores: Virgil rightly therefore uses 'severe' because they are sprung from hardy forbears [i.e. the Spartans] and because the Romans, when they were victorious followed their [the Sabines'] discipline in many ways.

59. Verona Scholia ad Verg. *Aen.* 7. 681

Cato in the *Origines* says that maidens seeking water found Caeculus at the hearth and therefore thought him the son of Vulcan. And because he had small eyes he was called Caeculus ['caecus', 'blind']. He gathered together shepherds and founded the city of Palestrina [Lat. Praeneste].

62. Serv. ad Verg. *Aen.* 11. 567

Though Metabus was of Privernum, yet because almost all Italy was in the power of the Etruscans the hatred of all was in general directed against Metabus. For he had been driven out by the tribe of the Volsci, which was itself ruled over by the Etruscans' power—which Cato has discussed very fully.

76. Serv. ad Verg. *Aen.* 9. 603

Virgil praises the discipline and life of Italy, which Cato in the *Origines* and Varro in the *De gente populi romani* recount.

77. Gell. 2. 28. 6

I do not choose to write what is recorded on the tablet at the pontifex maximus': how often corn was dear, how often darkness or something obscured the light of the moon.

83. Gell. 3. 7 (I quote only the exact citation, not the long Gellian paraphrase which sets the scene)

The immortal gods granted the military tribune a fate in keeping with his courage. It happened thus. Though he had been wounded in the battle in many places, yet there was no wound to his head and they identified him among the dead, unconscious because of his wound and from loss of blood. They carried him off and he recovered: often thereafter he performed brave and active service for the state and because he led that march to distract the Carthaginians he saved the rest of the army. But it makes a great deal of difference where you perform one and the same service. Leonidas the Spartan [who] did something similar at Thermopylae and on account of his virtues all Greece conferred on him exceptional thanks and honours, and decorated him with tributes to his most outstanding renown: with pictures, statues, inscriptions, histories, and in other ways they treated his deed as most welcome, but the tribune of the soldiers was left little praise for his deeds, though he did the same thing and saved the day.

88. Plin. *NH* 8. 11

To be sure, though Cato has removed the names of the generals from his annals, he records that the elephant which fought most bravely in the Carthaginians' battle-line was called 'the Syrian' and had one broken tusk.

92. Liv. 34. 15. 9 called Cato no belittler of his own praises.

95. Gell. 6. 3: his answer to the critique made by Cicero's freedman Tiro of Cato's speech in defence of the Rhodians, which like the attack on Servius Sulpicius Galba was included in the *Origines* (book 5). Gellius gives ten pages of the text of the speech.

118. Cic. *Tusc.* 4. 3

An author of great weight, Cato, in the *Origines*, said that it was our ancestors' custom at banquets that those who reclined sang, in sequence, to the flute, of the praises and virtues of famous men.

ATTICUS: SELECTED FRAGMENTS

Liber annalis

Fragments of Atticus' work are preserved ungenerously. I offer a selection translated from *HRR* ii. 6 ff.

3. Asc. ad Cic. *Corn.* p. 77. 2 ff. Clark
But some writers say that five tribunes of the people were then created, not two as Cicero says: one from each class. But there are those who say like Cicero that the number was two: for example Tuditanus, Pomponius Atticus, and Livy.

4. Cic. *Brut.* 42 (addressed to Atticus)
Since both of them (Themistocles and Coriolanus), though distinguished citizens, were banished by the injustice of an ungrateful people and quelled only by suicide the impulses born of their resentment. For though I know you have another account of the death of Coriolanus, do grant my preference for suicide.

5. ib. 72
But this Livius was the first to put on a play [at Rome] when C. Claudius, son of Caecus and Marcus Tuditanus were consuls [240 BC] in the year before Ennius was born and in the 514th after the foundation of the city, as our source says. For authorities differ about the dates. But Accius says that Livius was taken prisoner at the fall of Tarentum by Quintus Maximus, consul for the fifth time [209], thirty years after the date for his play that Atticus gives and we find in the old *commentarii*.

6. Asc. ad Cic. *Pis.* p. 13. 16 ff. Clark
They also say that a house was built at public expense for the son of King Antiochus when he was a hostage; so for example Atticus in his *Liber annalis*. It is said later to have belonged to Lucilius the poet.

7. Nep. *Hann.* 13

There is no agreement under which consuls Hannibal died; Atticus left it on record in his *Liber annalis* that it was under Marcus Claudius Marcellus and Quintus Fabius Labeo [183].

8. Cic. *Att.* 12. 23. 2

It is recorded in your *Liber annalis* under which consuls Carneades and that embassy came to Rome.

LETTER OF CORNELIA

Like N. himself in the *Cato* (3. 5), I am obliged here to summarize a much fuller discussion elsewhere.[1] These excerpts of a letter from Cornelia to her son the tribune C. Gracchus are preserved in the manuscripts of N. Why should they be, if they are from an authentic letter of Cornelia? Because, it is said, N. cites the original text in a life either, possibly, of Cornelia, or of Gaius, much as Suetonius cited original texts in some of his biographies of emperors and poets. Here, though, there is a difficulty: Suetonius cites extensively while he has privileged access as imperial librarian and does so because he is trained as lexicographer and antiquarian. When access ceases so, largely, do citations, which are not an essential element of biography, but, far more probably, a daring Suetonian innovation, inspired by his exciting discoveries in the imperial archives.[2] Exact citation of original texts by ancient authors occurs in specific and limited contexts.[3] Antiquarians, grammarians, and lexicographers (Varro, Asconius, Verrius Flaccus, for example) cite earlier authors exactly, without embarrassment; for historians it is unimaginable (cf. notably, Tacitus' treatment of Claudius' speech on the admission of some Gauls to the senate, which is also preserved almost intact on a bronze tablet at Lyon[4]), for citation of another author's exact words, or so it was believed, destroys the stylistic originality and independence of a work and mars its even texture. There is nothing to suggest that N. had the appetite for exact archival research that we find in early Suetonius, for example, or in Asconius; his hasty and inexact disposition naturally inclined him to favour the easy alternative of the loose citation or adapted paraphrase. Certainly his 'quotations' elsewhere are not of authentic and original documents in their correct form. N., that is, does nothing here to diminish our view of Suetonius' originality in the matter of citation, and we expect him to cite much as Sallust—an historian, not a biographer, but a close contemporary—cites. Sallust at least distinguishes between explicit paraphrase (*Jug.* 9. 1, 24. 1) and alleged citation (*Cat.* 34. 3, 44. 4); the letters Sallust 'cites' manifest both distinctively Sallustian and distinctively non-Sallustian features, the latter clearly intended to recapture the flavour of the

---

[1] *Athen.* 65 (1987), 231 ff. [2] Wallace-Hadrill (1983), 50 ff.
[3] Cf. G. B. Townend, *Herm.* 88 (1960), 98 ff. on citations of Greek in Suetonius.
[4] Tac. *Ann.* 11. 23. 1 ff.; *ILS* 212; conveniently both available in Lewis–Reinhold, *Roman Civilisation*, ii. 131 ff.

original. Letters of Cornelia survived in N.'s time and her general culture was greatly admired. But N., both by convention and by disposition, could never cite them except in altered and adapted form: altered, indeed, perhaps more than once, for he could well have found his originals not in a library or archive, but already adapted once in an annalist's narrative of the Gracchan period. Yet we must be clear: close study of the letters reveals nothing that cannot be of the second century BC. If N.'s ultimate originals were by Cornelia, they have been altered very discreetly; if they were not, then the author was very nearly a contemporary. It is possible that they belong to an optimate attempt to revalue Cornelia *c.* 100 BC, alongside the surviving statue base in honour of 'Cornelia Africani f[ilia], Gracchorum'.[5] Only one or just possibly two details in the text might seem to indicate that Cornelia is a little unlikely to be the author, but they are very far from decisive. We have therefore no means of saying whether or not Cornelia was the author of the excerpts' originals. She could have been: but heated argument will not solve the matter. All we can say with some certainty is that these texts are not exact citations of virgin second-century BC originals, though they fit irreproachably into a context of (say) 125–124 BC, when the politically active Cornelia could quite credibly have attempted publicly to discourage her only surviving son from following his brother Tiberius' path.

---

[5] *ILS* 68; Plin. *NH* 34. 31; Plut. *CG* 4; F. Coarelli in *Le Dernier Siècle de la république romaine* (Strasbourg 1978), 13 ff.

*A passage excerpted from the letter of Cornelia,
mother of the Gracchi, from the book of Cornelius Nepos
'On the Latin Historians'*

You will say that it is a fine thing to take vengeance on your enemies. That no man judges greater or finer than I do, but only if it may be pursued without damage to the state. But so far as that is not possible, long and surely shall our enemies not perish and they shall be as they are now, before the state be overwhelmed and perish.

The same, elsewhere: I would venture to take a solemn oath that, except for the men who killed Tiberius Gracchus, no enemy has given me so much trouble and toil as you have done because of these matters. You should rather have borne the part of all those children whom I had before and taken care that I should have the least possible anxiety in old age, that, whatever you did, you wanted it above all to meet my approval and that you thought it sinful to do anything of major importance against my views, especially since so little of my life remains. Cannot even the brevity of that period do anything to stop you opposing me and destroying the state? What respite will there ever be? Will our family ever desist from madness? Will bounds ever be set to it? Will we ever cease and make an end of troubles, both enduring them and inflicting them? Will we ever feel real shame at throwing the state into turmoil and confusion? But if that really cannot be, seek the tribunate when I am dead. As far as I am concerned, do what you will, when I shall not feel it. When I am dead you will sacrifice to me and invoke your parent's divine protector. Then will you not be ashamed to wish to pray to those divinities, whom living and present you treated as deserted and abandoned? May Jupiter above not allow you to continue thus, nor let such madness enter your mind. And if you do persevere, I fear that all your life long by your own fault you will incur so much toil that you will never be able to think well of your own self.

COMMENTARY

LIFE OF CATO

Excerpt. See p. 3 and note on *Letter of Cornelia* (**historians**) for texts falsely attributed to the *Latin Historians* in the MSS, and p. 33 for probably authentic fragments. Fr. 55 (on Philistus) probably belongs to the Greek companion volume. Cf. Geiger (1985), 96 ff. with caution. The life of Atticus is likewise from N.'s *Latin Historians*, explicitly (p. 8); the lives of the foreign generals (p. 29–30 for the preface) are not specifically attributed to N. in the MSS and this has caused difficulties; there is good sense in J. Geiger, *LCM* 7. 9 (1982), 134 ff.

1. 1. Marcus Cato. On the non-significant omission of the *nomen* or *gentilicium* (Porcius), cf. Balsdon (1979), 156; N. is under no pressure of style or convention to give all three parts. The *cognomen* Cato, 'sharp', 'acute', is distinctively Sabine.

native. The heroic M. Curius had once been a neighbour (cf. Cic. *Sen.* 55 and, delightfully embroidered, Plut. *Cat. mai.* 2. 1). A reference (*Orat.* fr. 128) to clearing Sabine rocks for the plough, and a literary tendency to idealize the Sabines, have tended to overshadow Tusculum as his formative environment, but that was most probably the home of Cato and his forbears (Astin (1978), 1 f.).

Tusculum. Probably from 381 BC the town enjoyed a rare and privileged position: its inhabitants were full Roman citizens. See *OCD*² s.v. *municipium*; E. T. Salmon, *Roman Colonisation* (London 1969), 49 f. Substantial remains survive in the Alban hills, three miles from Frascati.

young man. Cato was born in 234; his first campaign was in 217–216, and he was quaestor in 204.

Sabinum. There was little room for expansion at Tusculum. Cato's great-grandfather had served in the Roman cavalry and that suggests wealth, but in senatorial terms Cato was a 'new man' without ancestors of senatorial rank (Wiseman (1971), 108 ff.

father. 'A brave man and a good soldier', said his son (Plut. *Cat. mai.* 1. 1), and clearly of some means. Cf. notes on *Att.* 1. 1 (**Roman**

race, equestrian rank) for Atticus' equestrian forbears, likewise from the small old towns near Rome.

Flaccus. Cf. Plut. *Cat. mai.* 3. 1–4: elaborated, but the details correspond closely with the familiar etiquette of the first steps of patronage (Saller (1982), 8 ff.; Badian (1958), 10 f.). For Lucius Valerius Flaccus, son of the consul of 227, patrician and rather colourless, cf. Astin (1978), 9 f.

censor. They were consuls in 195 (see note on 2. 1, **Flaccus**), censors in 184 (see note on 2. 3, **severity**.

Perperna. M. Perperna, rather than Perpenna (consul 92, censor 86); cf. W. V. Harris, *Rome in Etruria and Umbria* (Oxford 1971), 226 f. He was born in 147 and died in 49. Pliny (*NH* 7. 156) thus cites him among examples of extreme longevity.

was . . . relating. Cf. (e.g.) Cic. *Rep.* 1. 27 for this popular historiographical mannerism, lending vivacity and evoking continuity (M. Rambaud, *Cicéron et l'histoire* (Paris 1953), 104 ff.; Cic. *Brut.* (ed. A. E. Douglas), 6 ff.).

take . . . life. Literally 'to be in the forum'; apparently he had had some experience as a country pleader, supposedly in his late teens (Plut. *Cat. mai.* 3. 1; Astin (1978), 8). This was not unparalleled, even in the Roman forum (Taylor (1964), 29), though it has been supposed that the move to Rome did not come till Cato was in his late twenties; for a compromise solution see Scullard (1973), 256.

1. 2. age of seventeen. As Cato himself said (Plut. *Cat. mai.* 1. 6). Was it 216 rather than 217? See Astin (1978), 6 n. 13: he possibly first entered the Roman army in the special levy after the disastrous defeat at Cannae.

consulship. The standard method of dating in use at Rome (Bickerman (1968), 69, 77).

Q. Fabius and M. Claudius. Quintus Fabius Maximus and Marcus Claudius Marcellus were consuls in 214; Cato served in the former's army first in Campania (Cic. *Sen.* 10), then in Sicily (Astin (1978), 7 n. 14).

tribune. Promotion to military tribune in time of crisis could be almost immediate (cf. Horace in 43 BC!); that in turn would help at the elections. The rules regarding age and length of service in the army could clearly be suspended (Wiseman (1971), 121 f., 143 ff.; Scullard (1973), 110 f.).

Sicily. Cf. Liv. 24. 27. 6 for Marcellus' arrival in Sicily; cf. Lazenby (1978), 101 ff. for an admirably lucid account.

staff. Literally 'followed the camp', again presumably as military tribune. It is not clear when Cato's service in Sicily ended, or whether he also served at the capture of Tarentum (209; Scullard (1973), 111).

Nero. Cf. Hor. *Carm*. 4. 4. 37 ff.; he had had an undistinguished military career hitherto, but cf. Lazenby (1978), 185 ff. for his dogged campaign against Hannibal in the south, swift march to join his colleage Salinator, skilled command of the cavalry in the battle, and triumph.

Sena. The battle we call 'Metaurus' (so Liv. 27. 47. 9; Horace, loc. cit.), but many ancient authors referred like N. to 'Sena', ten miles to the south and just north of Ancona (e.g. Cic. *Brut*. 73). It is not clear where the battle took place (Walbank on Plb. 11. 1 ff.; Lazenby (1978), 188). Perhaps yet another battle delocalized because of terminological confusion between 'left' and 'right' banks of a river (Horsfall, *G&R* 32 (1985), 204 f.).

Hasdrubal. His march through France alerted the Romans and his message to Hannibal was intercepted (Lazenby (1978), 181 ff.).

killed. C. Claudius Nero marched swiftly back south and delivered Hasdrubal's head to his brother's camp (Lazenby (1978), 190).

1. 3. quaestor. N. here suggests (as at 2. 2) that Cato was elected quaestor in 205; 1. 4 points to 204, the date elsewhere attested (*MRR* i. 310; Astin (1978), 12). N. may be writing loosely here, but the accounts available to him may not have been consistent.

allotted. For the sortition of provinces, as in the case of consuls and praetors, cf. L. A. Thompson, *Hist.* 11 (1962), 339 ff., who explains how the chance of sortition imposes a special bond.

P. Africanus. The future Africanus; cf. Plut. *Cat. mai.* 3. 5–8, our only account in detail, much of it not credible.

life. Notably in the 180s. Plutarch (loc. cit.) probably and N. possibly retroject later disagreements (Astin (1978), 13 ff.; *contra*, Scullard (1973), 112; id., *Scipio Africanus* (London 1970), 187 ff.). Cf. further p. 4 n. 9. Cf. Powell on Cic. *Sen.* 19.

aedile. In 199; he and Helvius found means to extend the number of games performed (Astin (1978), 20), and were duly elected praetors for the following year.

1. 4. occasion. N., for brevity, inserts an awkward flashback; the *De viris illustribus* (in this case, the *c*.4 AD biographical handbook) 52. 3 conflates the two visits. But see E. Badian, *Entr. Hardt*, 17 (1971), 157 f. and *CPh* 80 (1985), 346 n. 5, who describes the story that Cato brought Ennius from Sardinia as 'an ancient myth'.

Africa. Details of his service there are unclear (Liv. 29. 25. 10), as are the date of his return (between 204 and 202) and his motive for visiting Sardinia.

home. Ennius praised Cato to the skies (Cic. *Arch.* 22; Skutsch (1985), 642 f.). Cato, according to N., took Ennius to Rome. The poet (b. 239) was a native of Rudiae in Calabria: had he been serving in Sardinia in an allied contingent (Skutsch (1985), 1)?

poet. If Silius (12. 393 ff.: a warrior from Rudiae called Ennius) refers to the poet Ennius, which is most unlikely, it has no value as evidence. The *De viris illustribus* (47. 1) perhaps rightly says that Ennius taught Cato Greek; but see note on 3. 2, **Greek . . . affairs**. Fifteen years later (Cic. *Tusc.* 1. 3), Cato criticized M. Fulvius Nobilior for taking Ennius on campaign.

value. Cf. p. xix for the tone of heavily explicit moral evaluation; but N. is quite right to see in Ennius' arrival at Rome a moment of great importance in cultural history (cf. Astin (1978), 17; Gratwick *CHCL* ii. 75 f.): epic and tragedy are given a powerful new impetus and imperial expansion acquires its laureate.

Sardinia. Cf. Astin (1978), 20 f. for the little that is known of Cato's honest and frugal governorship. The author of the *De viris illustribus* (see note on 1. 4, **occasion**) unfortunately also says that Cato subjugated Sardinia; his turn of office was uneventful and the encounter with Ennius conveniently fills a void.

2. 1. Flaccus. Cf. note on 1. 1, **Flaccus**. Valerius had been praetor the year before Cato, and like Cato had used lavish games put on as aedile to woo the voters. In 198 Cato had drawn the dull province; this time, Valerius Flaccus campaigned inconclusively in northern Italy (Cisalpine Gaul) (Astin (1978), 28).

Hither Spain. From Saragossa to Almeria and from Toledo to the sea; but neither Cato nor P. Manlius in Hispania Ulterior kept rigidly to their boundaries.

province. On Cato's campaigns cf. Richardson (1986), 79 ff.; Astin (1978), 28 ff. 'A great general' says N. (see note on 3. 1, **general**); one of his more defensible exaggerations.

triumph. This was well earned. Cato did not play down his achievements (Astin (1978), 52 f.; Richardson (1986), 88 f.); hence there is an exceptionally full account at some removes in Livy.

2. 2. too long. It does appear from Plut. *Cat. mai.* 11 (cf. Astin (1978), 51 f.) that Cato was criticized for actions taken against the Lacetani after he had formally been replaced.

second time. In 194; for his first consulship cf. note on 1. 3 (**quaestor**). It is unlikely that N. gives a correct account. Plutarch (*Cat. mai.* 11) says Scipio went to Spain. Was N. confused by the (different) P. Scipio Nasica who served in Ulterior in 194? See Richardson (1986), 90; Astin (1978), 51 f.

in person. Livy more credibly says that it was to Macedonia that Scipio wanted to go (34. 43. 4). Cf. Scullard, *Scipio Africanus*, 283 f.

senate. N. realizes that the position of a *princeps* was in the 190s licit and compatible with senatorial authority. He has seen and here obliquely deplores (cf. *Att.* 20. 5) a remarkable growth in the power an individual *princeps* might exercise; cf. Syme (1939), 311; Cic. *Rep.* 1. 68 on 'the excessive power of the *principes*' (note on *Att.* 20. 5, **prizes**).

state. Scullard (1973), 110 ff. on 'the Scipionic recovery' should be viewed with great caution. Many Cornelii held curule office in the 190s, but the *gens* was huge and many of its members were not recognizably kin of the Scipiones.

law. This was a familiar accusation against (e.g.) Julius Caesar (Cic. *Off.* 3. 83) and Mark Antony (Cic. *Phil.* 8. 8); cf. Ps. Sall. *Ep. ad Caes.* 2. 5. 3 for the conflict of *potentia* and *leges*, and Sall. *Oratio Lepidi* 4: in the third and second centuries, there was obedience to the law. For a similar lament cf. *Ages.* 4. 2 and *Att.* 6. 2.

office. The consuls were assigned Italy; Scipio in fact did little (Scullard, *Scipio Africanus*, 194; id. (1973), 118).

2. 3. severity. Cato was censor in 184, having failed in the elections of 189 (Astin (1978), 78 ff.; Scullard (1973), 153 ff.): a tenure of office characterized by 'acerbitas' (Liv. 39. 44. 9).

took action. In contrast to the relatively tolerant censorships of 194 and 189 (Astin (1978), 88), seven members of the senate were expelled and numerous *equites* (see note on *Att.* 1. 1, **equestrian rank**) were deprived of their status, with or without ignominy (Scullard (1973), 157 f.). For Cato's hostility towards the obese cf. Gell. 6. 22. 1; Plut. *Cat. mai.* 9. 6.

nobles. These included the brother of Scipio Africanus (cf. note on 2. 2, **second time**). But despite (e.g.) Livy's epigrammatic verdict (39. 40. 9), there are inadequate grounds for supposing that Cato was systematically opposed to the aristocracy: cf. Astin (1978), 66 f.

edict. The censors on taking office set forth in an edict the principles they would follow (J. Suolahti, *The Roman Censors* (Helsinki 1963), 355; Scullard (1973), 156). On luxury Cato speaks from the heart; he is memorable and irresistible to moralizing historians and biographers, and this creates a certain imbalance in the record. Cf. A. W. Lintott, *Hist.* 21 (1972), 631 ff.

already. Cato's attacks go back long before his censorship; cf. note on 1. 3 (**life**), for the attack on Scipio, if authentic ('corrupting the native frugality of his soldiers'). See Astin (1978), 25 ff.) for his opposition to the repeal of the *lex Oppia* during his consulship, and Plut. *Cat. mai.* 16. 6 f. (with Astin (1978), 75 ff.) for his campaign for election as censor, with promises of exceptional severity.

beginning to sprout. An agricultural metaphor, arguably borrowed by N. from Cato himself, the author of a surviving manual on farming (see note on 3. 1, **farmer**).

2. 4. about eighty years. The facts are striking enough but N., innumerate, generalizes ineptly: Cato died at the age of 83, and the approximate life-span is transferred unthinkingly to the length of Cato's political activity.

republic. Cf. Livy's verdicts (39. 40. 8, 39. 44. 9). Cato was forty-four times accused and acquitted, and was frequently also an accuser (Astin (1978), 105 ff.). Astin (1978), 111 f. shows that he was very ready to play on his old age, attacking Servius Sulpicius Galba, aged 83 (note on 3. 4, **Galba . . . Lusitanians**). Cf. note on *Att*. 11. 5 (**he . . . avenge**) on feuds in public life, so carefully avoided by Atticus.

reputation. But notice that Livy (see previous note) and Plutarch (e.g. *Cat. mai.* 15. 4) preserve reactions of dismay at his litigiousness.

attracted. Cf. Liv. 34. 15. 9; Plut. *Cat. mai.* 14. 2; see Astin (1978), 295 ff. for the development of the overwhelmingly sympathetic literary tradition about him. But inevitably he attracted criticism; cf. note on 1.ˉ3 (**life**) for Scipio, with Astin (1978), 109.

3. 1. farmer. There is a convenient Loeb edition of Cato on agriculture, a handbook on large-scale estate management; cf. Astin (1978), 189 ff.; K. D. White, *Roman Farming* (London 1970), 19 f. Cato's book is peremptory, chaotic, indigestible, and often erroneous. On the problems of the panegyric of farming put into Cato's mouth at Cic. *Sen.* 51–60 cf. Astin (1978), 297 f.; E. Rawson, *JRS* 62 (1972), 39 f.: Cato pasteurized and homogenized, but recognizable if not always unchallengeably authoritative. Cf. Plut. *Cat. mai.* 21. 5 on how Cato really made his money; he may have taken farming less seriously in old age: cf. Astin (1978), 249 f.

lawyer. Cicero (*Sen.* 38) refers to Cato in old age as writing on the civil law, especially about augurs and pontiffs; cf. Astin (1978), 185. N.'s account of Cato's skills clearly derives from a glance at the titles of Cato's works.

general. Cf. Astin (1978), 6, 49. Numerous laudatory assessments (e.g. Cic. *Sen.* 32) do not quite square with the record: Cato's triumph appears rather easily earned. There is no question of his courage or endurance, nor of his tactical competence (cf. Astin (1978), 184 f. for his manual *De re militari*). But, his own publicity aside, how much more?

orator. On Cato's speeches cf. p. 35. Conventionalized but defensible assessments of a remarkable man inevitably, but in part unfairly, incur suspicion on account of N.'s dithyrambic tone; *Att.* 16. 4.

3. 2. older man. Cf. note on 1. 4 (**poet**) on when he took seriously to Greek. Cato reached the peak of his public career at 50 and lived for another thirty years; cf. note on Cato, frr. 1–3 for the Roman preoccupation with the justification of leisure pursuits. Cato's later years were contemporary with the literary activity of Ennius, Caecilius and Terence; Latin prose literature was his own creation (Gratwick, *CHCL* ii. 149 ff.).

anything. Cato's range is likewise overestimated at Liv. 39. 40. 7; Plut. *Cat. mai.* 25. 1; cf. *Att.* 16. 4 for N. in a similar vein on Cicero's letters. Even if Cato's *Ad filium* is not a sort of encyclopaedia of practical knowledge (Gratwick, *CHCL* ii. 827; Astin (1978), 332 ff.), the range (cf. following note) remains very considerable (Gratwick *CHCL* ii. 826 ff.; Astin (1978), 182 ff.); exaggeration was unnecessary.

Greek . . . affairs. Plutarch (*Cat. mai.* 2. 5) shows that a Greek recognized numerous allusions to Greek literature in Cato's writings, and it is clear that he could quote Homer in public (Plb. 36. 8. 7, 35. 6. 3 f.; cf. Astin (1978), 162 ff.). Greek he may have learned from Ennius; serious interest in literature came from a good deal later (Val. Max. 8. 7. 1; Astin (1978), 159). On philosophy, he was apparently no keener than (p. xvi) N. himself (Gell. 18. 7. 3, Plut. *Cat. mai.* 23. 1; Astin (1978), 169 f.). But historians, tacticians, and agronomists he probably consulted extensively; see note on Nepos, fr. 56.

3. 3. speeches. Cf. note on 1. 1 (**take . . . life**) on the beginning of his career as a public speaker and p. 35 on the surviving fragments.

old man. Cf. Cic. *Sen.* 38; fr. 49 is not earlier than 168 (cf. note on 3. 4, **in the same way**); book 7 included the speech against Servius Sulpicius Galba (cf. note on *Cato*, 3. 4, **Galba . . . Lusitanians**), of the last year of his life (149).

histories. Note that he also himself wrote out 'in large letters' a history for his son, to teach him about 'things old and national' (Plut. *Cat. mai.* 20. 7; Astin (1978), 182 f.).

survive. Cf. Astin (1978), 211 ff.; Gratwick, *CHCL* ii. 149 ff.; and notably Badian (1966), 7 ff. For translation and comment on some fragments of the seven books cf. pp. 36–8, 121–3.

first. Cf. frr. 1, 2, 3, 17, 21 Peter; the book in fact refers to events both before Aeneas and after the kings (fr. 25: cf. Liv. 3. 18: 460 BC).

second and third. Cf. frr. 31, 32, 34, 49, 51, 59, 62 (pp. 121–2).

communities. Note that Cato writes of both towns and peoples; and it will be clear even from the selection translated that the range of books 2–3 was a good deal wider than N.'s summary suggests.

Italy. The fragments translated give some idea of the geographical range, though it is not clear how far Cato had an idea of Italy as a geographical unity: cf. fr. 85 'the Alps, which according to Cato and Livy (21. 35. 8) protect Italy like a wall' (cf. Plin. *NH* 3. 132). The range of Cato's Italian foundation-legends can hardly be dissociated from his perception of the impact of the Hannibalic war on the entire peninsula, and his vision of history as Italian, not Roman, remained unique.

called. N.'s statement that *Origines* was Cato's own title is perhaps true, though many ancient statements about authentic authorial titulature are not (cf. Horsfall, *BICS* 28 (1981), 103 f.). N. is here confirmed by the lexicographer Festus and by the uniformity of the citations. Perhaps most important, the title bears the unmistakable stamp of Catonian individuality, though this was the first work of Latin historiography!

Origines. The title is much more appropriate to the first three books than to the remainder; cf. Astin (1978), 219. *Origines* does not exactly translate the Greek *ktiseis* ('foundations'), nor is it well rendered by 'genealogies' (D.H. 1. 1. 1). Cf. Astin (1978), 227 ff. for a too rigorously sceptical view of Cato's relationship to near-contemporary Greek writing on the foundation of cities; *c*.4–3 BC Greeks wrote amply about Italian foundation stories (T. J. Cornell, *PCPhS* 21 (1975), 19 f., 23 f.).

first Punic war. Took place 264–241, but fr. 84 refers to 219 BC, fr. 85 (see note on 3. 3, **Italy**) presumably to 218, and fr. 86 to 216, after Cannae.

the second. A similar problem: 'second Punic war' (218–201) is a
straitjacket that again does not fit, for fr. 92 refers to 195 and fr. 95
(p. 38) to 167.

3. 4. summarily. So Astin (1978), 218, argues against Badian
(1966), 8, 'by subject-matter'. N.'s meaning here is hotly debated,
but in a closely parallel passage the elder Pliny uses 'capitulatim' as
a synonym of 'breviter', briefly (2. 55). In N.'s text the adverb
applies explicitly to Cato's books 4–5 and by extension ('in the same
way') to books 6–7. In the later books, though (p. 122–3), some
episodes were clearly treated much more amply: note the (probably)
detailed narrative of Cato's Spanish campaign, the episode of
Caedicius (p. 37), and the inclusion (see notes on 3. 4, **in the same
way, Galba**) of at least two of Cato's own speeches. How and where
Cato treated the early republic is not clear (Astin (1978), 215 ff.). In
Greek, Fabius Pictor had done so 'summarily' (D.H. 1. 6. 2).

in the same way. But Livy (45. 25. 3) says that Cato's speech (p.
38) on behalf of the Rhodians (167 BC) was included in book 5. Was
he right? Is N.'s summary correct? One expects inaccuracy in
summaries: cf. Propertius' of Ennius, 3. 3. 1–14 (Skutsch (1985),
15 f.; but see S. J. Heyworth *CQ* 36 (1986), 200 f.). The *Periochae* of
Livy (P. Jal, *Tite-Live*, ed. Budé 34. 1 (Paris 1984), pp. xxxix ff.) and
the epitomes of Homer (Horsfall, *JHS* 99 (1979), 34, 45 f.) are also
untrustworthy. The questions here posed must remain unanswered.

Galba . . . Lusitanians. In 150 BC, despite undertakings, he
massacred a large number and enslaved the remainder (Scullard
(1973), 234 ff.). But at his trial the following year bribery and
sentiment (cf. Cic. *De orat.* 1. 228: 'he lifted up his ward Quintus
almost up to his shoulders') proved more powerful than Cato's
eloquence (Astin (1978), 111 ff.)!

by name. Can this have been quite true? Cf. Astin (1978), 213;
cf. note on Cato, fr. 88 for the exceptional elephant.

without names. Cf. fr. 83 (p. 123) and Astin (1978), 217. Was this
related to the view attributed to Cato (though not explicitly to the
Origines) by Cicero (*Rep.* 2. 2) that Rome's greatness was not the
work of one man (such as Minos, Lycurgus, or Solon), but of many?
Cf. Griffin (1985), 178 ff. on Rome as a collective state. Or was Cato
protesting as a new man against the aristocratic monopoly of
achievement? Or as an historian against the lies and exaggerations

engendered by the traditions and records of the individual *gentes*? Cf.
Horsfall, *BICS* 30 (1983), 89 f.

events and sights. See also frr. 78, 80 (Africa), frr. 96, 97
(Illyricum). Varro (*Fundanius de admirandis*), Cicero (a lost *De
admirandis*), and the elder Pliny (e.g. 31. 12, 51) used *admiranda* of
natural phenomena (cf. Geiger (1985), 72). Cato's scope and
curiosity were much wider ranging: though oddity is one reason for
preservation, with the result that our impression is inevitably
loaded, the surviving fragments suggest that the *Origines*—didactic
moralizing (fr. 83) and pioneer ethnography aside—conveyed an
extraordinary rag-bag of information.

Italy and Spain. Italy: frr. 76 (cf. p. 37), 118 (cf. p. 38), 119, 120,
134; Spain: frr. 94, 110.

learning. Did Cato not name sources? Or discuss alternative
versions? Cf. Astin (1978), 223. By comparison with Varro's
recently issued *Antiquitates* (25 books on human affairs and 16 on
divine), which had so awed Cicero (*Ac. Post.* 1. 9; Horsfall *BICS* 19
(1972), 120 ff.; and id., *CHCL* ii. 289), Cato's *Origines* may indeed
have seemed unscholarly, but one might wonder whether N. was
quite the proper person to make such disdainful comments. N. may,
however, refer only to the absence of Greek scientific theory in the
Admiranda (see note on 3. 4, **events and sights**).

3. 5. separate study. This was presumably used by Plutarch (J.
Geiger, *Herm.* 109 (1981), 97; Astin (1978), 299 f.). But decisive
proofs are lacking and the coincidences between N.'s shorter life that
we have and Plutarch have also been explained (e.g.) by common
use of Polybius.

Atticus. Perhaps after the younger Cato's suicide (46 BC) and before
beginning the *De viris illustribus*. Atticus was close both to Cato and
to Cato's son-in-law Brutus, whose family he himself studied (see
note on *Att.* 18. 3, **present**). Distinguish Maecenas' 'iussa' to Virgil
to write the *Georgics* (*G.* 3. 41) from Atticus' 'rogatus': 'order' against
'request', roughly, in keeping with N.'s status relative to Atticus.

LIFE OF ATTICUS

1. 1. Atticus. Cicero (*Sen.* 1) says that Atticus brought back from Greece (see note on 4. 5, **consuls**) 'humanitas' (4. 1, **Athens**), 'prudentia' (16. 4, **for . . . state**), and 'cognomen' (Atticus); for the rarely-used full form of his name cf. note on 5. 2 (**three-quarters**).

Roman race. Does N. here hint at a fine flourish of genealogical inventiveness? The Calpurnii claimed descent from King Numa's son Calpus, the Pomponii from his brother Pompo: cf. T. P. Wiseman, *G&R* 21 (1974), 154 f.; Brink on Hor. *AP* 322. But Atticus was Rome's leading exponent of genealogical rigour (see note on 18. 3, **families**) and would hardly have suggested or appreciated such fantasies; equestrian rank did not rule out long and credible pedigrees (Gelzer (1969), 17 f.); for Cato, cf. note on *Cato*, 1. 1 (**Sabinum**).

equestrian rank. 'The cream of the notably heterogeneous equestrian Order' (Wiseman (1971), 68 ff.), qualified not only by property (amply over the necessary 400,000 HS) but passed by the censors as eligible to vote in the equestrian centuries in the *comitia centuriata* (I. Henderson, *JRS* 53 (1963), 61 ff. = Seager (1969), 69 ff.). Atticus too is satisfied with his *dignitas* (see note on *Att.* 2. 2, **standing**), declines office (6. 2 with notes), avoids active participation in public life, like many others of his rank (see note on 5. 4, **waves of the sea**; SB i. 5; Syme (1939), 517), and leaves startlingly swift upward mobility to his immediate descendants (see note on 19. 2, **entered**).

1. 2. rich. A sharp passing observation: Atticus is born before large estates, exports of wine and oil, regular large-scale campaigning, and exploitation in the provinces vastly increase levels of income (Frank, *ESAR* i. 295 ff.): before the evidence of Cicero, unfortunately, only exceptional wealth is recorded in detail (cf. Cic. *Rep.* 3. 13, Frank, *ESAR* i. 299). One notes a similar sharp awareness of social change at *Att.* 13 f. and in the *Exempla* (p. xviii n. 18).

instructed. Did Atticus' father teach his son? That is what the text says, and N. tells us that his father was industrious and a lover of literature (cf. further note on 2. 4, **father**). Teaching at home was the old Roman style: cf. note on *Cato*, 3. 3 (**histories**) for Cato. But

we know (see note on *Att.* 1. 4, **Torquatus . . . Cicero**) that Atticus
also went to 'school'; the information is not incompatible.

in all . . . share. N.'s laborious high-mindedness is at times
indigestible and it is easy to see why, despite his tolerance (see note
on *Foreign Generals*, 2, **morality**), he so appealed (p. xix n. 23) to
later generations of educators.

1. 3. extremely well. Cf. 4. 1 with notes. Cicero compliments
Atticus (*Leg.* 2. 45) on his wonderful memory; it had been properly
trained, as N. implies here; cf. Cic. *Leg.* 2. 59 (XII Tables!); Aug.
Conf. 1. 13. 20 (Virgil); Quint. 1. 1. 36 (anthologies), 11. 2. 40 f.;
Marrou (1956), 279; Bonner (1977), 225 f. As a reader, Virgil
himself attracted similar admiration (*Vit. Don.* 28); the terms of N.'s
compliment are perhaps (Ramage (1973), 106 f.) borrowed from
Cicero (*De orat.* 3. 42; cf. p. 12–13 for clearer examples of such
indebtedness).

equanimity. N. does not imply that the swot Atticus was bullied by
his exasperated contemporaries; rather, as did Cicero (Plut. *Cic.*
2. 2; cf. Bonner (1977), 135), he inspired them to healthy emulation.

1. 4. Torquatus . . . Cicero. There is no hint that Atticus went
anywhere between domestic instruction and joining the illustrious
circle of adolescents whose studies were overseen by L. Licinius
Crassus the orator; he then passed to legal studies with Crassus'
father-in-law Q. Mucius Scaevola Augur. Crassus engaged outside
help (e.g. Archias): see Cic. *De orat.* 2. 2; E. Rawson, *PCPhS* 17
(1971), 82 f.; Bonner (1977), 76 f.; Mitchell (1979), 6. A prescient
father ensures that Atticus makes invaluable friendships early.
Cicero he probably does not meet until they are students of
Scaevola; indeed it is not formally attested (merely, I think, likely)
that Atticus went to Crassus; the young Marius he helps soon (see
note on 2. 2, **enemy . . . state aid**), Q. Gellius Kanus (10. 2 with
notes) nearly half a century later. Lucius Manlius Torquatus
becomes consul in 65 and dies *c.*53; Atticus has other friends in the
family (SB i. 8; see note on 11. 2, **A. Torquatus**).

captivated . . . lives. Atticus' exceptional charm and capacity for
inspiring friendship is a motif of the whole work (1. 4, 2. 4, 3. 1, 5. 1,
9. 3, etc.), as it is in Horace (in both the *Carmina* and *Epodes*, R. G. M.
Nisbet and M. Hubbard, *A Commentary on Horace*: Odes (Oxford
1970), vol. i. p. xxi). It will also emerge that N. has in mind the
Ciceronian ideal of friendship (*Lael.*; cf. p. 12).

2. 1. father. Beyond what N. tells us (1. 2), we learn (Cic. *Leg.* 3. 49; Rawson (1985), 234) that Atticus' father was the dedicatee of a work on the powers of the magistracies; his mother was a sister of the immensely rich equestrian financier Q. Caecilius (cf. further note on 5. 1, **Quintus Caecilius**).

Sulpicius. In 88 as *tribunus plebis* he introduced, amid scenes of violence, legislation to enrol the new Italian citizens fairly and to replace Sulla with Marius in the command against Mithridates. Sulla (with his fellow-consul) was expelled from Rome but returned with an army, and Sulpicius was shortly put to death. Cf. E. Badian, *Hist.* 18 (1969), 481 ff.; *MRR* ii. 41 f.; A. Keaveney, *Lat.* 38 (1979), 451 ff.

Sulpicius' brother. Cicero (*Lael.* 2) suggests close association between Atticus and Sulpicius. Anicia's mother will have been a sister of Atticus' father; her father Anicius was of an old Praenestine family. This brother of P. Sulpicius is otherwise unknown. Cf. Nicolet, ii (1974), 989.

2. 2. Cinna. In 87, Cinna (cf. note on 2. 1, **Sulpicius**) was declared *hostis*, enemy of Rome, though a *tumultus Italicus* may not formally have been decreed, placing Rome on a war footing as in 63 (Catiline) and 49 (Caesar). Cf. note on 9. 2 (**left Italy**) for a similar problem. The schematized sequence 'Sulpicius . . . Cinna . . . is typical of the way Rome's civil wars and disturbances are presented: cf. Jal (1963), 43 ff.

standing. *Dignitas*, an important word to N., and therefore perhaps to Atticus too: (cf. also 6. 2; 19. 2; 21. 1, with note on **influence**). See Wistrand (1978), 29: 'the word connotes a man's rank and prestige in society . . . acquired through noble birth and personal achievements . . . the word also implies . . . that you are worthy of something.' Cf. too C. Wirszubski, *JRS* 44 (1954), 12 = Seager (1969), 194, and id. *Libertas* (Cambridge 1960), 36; Brunt, *JRS* 76, (1986) 15 f.

other. N.'s polarized view (cf. 7. 1, 3; 8. 4–5; 9. 2–3; 10. 1; 20. 5) is conventional (cf. note on 8. 4, **conspiratorial**) but justifiable; cf. Brunt, *JRS* 58 (1968), 231 f.

Cinna. He returned to Rome in late 87 with an army, repealed Sulla's laws, and killed many of his supporters. His *dominatio* lasted until his violent death in early 84: 'no arms were drawn at Rome; orators died, left, or fled' (Cic. *Brut.* 308). Sulla throughout this period was in the East. Velleius (2. 24. 4) speaks of the three years during which the *partes* (see note on 8. 4, **conspiratorial**) of Marius and Cinna controlled Italy. Senators (Plut. *Sulla*, 22. 1) joined Sulla in Greece to escape Cinna and Carbo, as did Atticus: cf. E. Badian, *JRS* 52 (1962), 47 ff = *Studies in Greek and Roman History* (Oxford 1964), 206 f.; C. M. Bulst, *Hist.* 13 (1964), 318 ff.

Athens. It is not quite clear (cf. note on 4. 1, **Athens**) when Atticus went to Greece, nor when he left (cf. note on 4. 5, **consuls**); Cicero was there 79–77; see the charming picture in *Fin.* 5. 1–5, also *Brutus* 315; Rawson (1985), 9, and (1975), 26 ff.; SB i. 4.

enemy of the state. Atticus' loyalty to his 'schoolfellows' is an important theme (cf. 4. 4, 5. 3, 10. 3); Cicero was distant kin to the young Marius but never claims acquaintance (Mitchell (1979), 8) though this passage suggests it existed. About 93 the young Marius married Licinia, daughter of his and Atticus' educator, Crassus; her mother was the daughter of their other teacher Scaevola (see note on 1. 4, **Torquatus**). In 88 it was only Scaevola, according to Valerius Maximus (3. 8. 5), who protested against Sulla's brutal haste. Marius sent his son to hide at Scaevola's house; the son spent the night at his wife's and then fled to Africa: ample detail is available (T. F. Carney, *G&R* 8 (1961), 103); N. has been missed, and the speed of their flight suggests that Atticus was there in Rome and gave help during a day of perilous emergency.

help. That Atticus helps his friends above all in their times of distress is a recurrent theme: cf. 4. 4, 7. 1, 8. 6 (**in desperate straits**), 11. 1.

2. 3. moved . . . Athens. On the mechanisms that existed for transferring money cf. Bonner (1977), 91 and the discussions of Hellenistic banking cited in note on 2. 4 (**he . . . fixed**). To judge by the scale of Atticus' later business activities in the Aegean (see note on 14. 3, **income**), he will already have been busy enlarging the fairly modest inheritance received from his father.

for good reason. Cf. 4. 5 (**escorted**) and 22. 4 (**men of substance**) for public displays of the affection that Atticus inspired at large.

2. 4. own resources. Atticus (cf. note on 1. 1) was a public benefactor of Athens on a scale far beyond that justified by his patrimony (14. 2) of 2 million HS; other sources of income are the inescapable conclusion (cf. note on 14. 3, **income**). This was a time (see following note) of desperate need for the Athenians and they rewarded Atticus only too amply.

when . . . terms. Especially after Aristion's tyranny and the sack of Athens by Sulla in 86. Athens was not likely to be thought worthy of credit on generous terms. But Atticus stopped the Athenians from having to accept severe terms by 'stepping in', that is, by raising the money himself and passing on the favourable terms that he could himself obtain to the Athenians, asking no further interest for himself, but requiring the Athenians to meet the terms that he had been offered. For this admirable explanation (made in 1836!), cf. Drumann v². 12 n. 4; for the same procedure again cf. note on 9. 5 (**stepped . . . terms**).

he . . . fixed. For private individuals lending to cities cf. Frank, *ESAR* i. 388; Atticus' generosity was not unparalleled (Hill (1952), 83). Athens was normally teeming with Roman bankers (Larsen, *ESAR* iv. 360 f.; Keaveney (1982), 125) but will have been delighted to get out of their hands; for though Atticus may have had to pass on 12 per cent interest, they would themselves have received far less generous terms (Rostovtzeff (1953), 959 f.; Frank, *ESAR* i. 352). For the world of Hellenistic banking cf. Rostovtzeff (1953), 1278 ff.; F. M. Heichelheim, *Ancient Economic History*, iii (Leiden 1970), 112 ff.

2. 5. interest. Cf. note on 2. 4 (**when . . . terms**).

2. 6. per head. For the measure (about 40 kg.) see R. P. Duncan Jones, *Economy of the Roman Empire*² (Cambridge 1982), 370 f. Cicero was a good deal surprised when Atticus made a donation of corn at Athens in 50 (*Att.* 6. 6. 2), but accepted it as 'generosity towards hosts' rather than 'largesse towards fellow-countrymen'. Plutarch has left a grim account of the siege conditions in Athens in 87–6 (*Sulla*, 13).

medimnus. Plautus might use 'medimnus' to his theatre public unexplained (*St.* 587); N. writing consciously to communicate to the uninformed (cf. p. xix) is careful to give the equivalent dry measure.

3. 1. seem. Cf. note on 2. 3 (**for good reason**). N. is notably concerned with the impressions that Atticus gave to others (1. 4, 2. 3, 4. 1, 9. 5, 10. 5, 10. 6, 12. 5, 15. 2), a technique of characterization also familiar in historians (P. G. Walsh, *Livy* (Cambridge 1961), 82 f.).

all . . . possible. Rewards such as a crown, free meals for life, front seats for athletic and dramatic performances, for example; cf. S. Dow, *HSCP* 67 (1963), 81 ff., a reference for which I am grateful to D. M. Lewis. Cf. also A. R. Hands, *Charities and Social Aid* (London 1968), 49 ff.

take advantage. Following this the MSS of N. include the words 'he was unwilling because some interpret the matter thus, that Roman citizenship is lost if another is acquired.' Of the period of Atticus' residence at Athens (say 85–65) this was clearly true (cf. Cic. *Balb.* 28, 30, *Caec.* 100; Balsdon (1979), 97) though the rule about holding office in two cities was being relaxed (A. N. Sherwin-White, *Roman Citizenship*[2] (Oxford 1973), 303). By the time N. wrote, this fundamental 'rule' of Roman citizenship had almost collapsed and the attribution to N. of the words quoted might be defended by construing them as comment on the confused and ambiguous time at which he was writing (cf. E. Rawson, *Athen.* 63 (1985), 56 f.). But the phrasing of the disputed words is notably awkward and I doubt that N. wrote them.

3. 2. statues. If this is really what N. wrote (it is an attractive emendation by Wagner, no more; *et fidie* is in the MSS); possibly a reference to Atticus' wife Pilia (see note on 4. 3, **head of a household**) lurks here; or to his daughter Caecilia (cf. note on 12. 2, **marriage**). Clearly the sculptor Phidias (active 450–30 BC) is irrelevant. A fragment of the dedication of a statue of Atticus to the Eleusinian deities by the daughter of his teacher Phaedrus (cf. note on 12. 3, **Lucius Saufeius**) survives (*IG* ii[2]. 3513) but does not help resolve the problem here (cf. Raubitschek, *Hesp.* 18 (1949), 102 with caution). The precise location of a statue could determine the degree of honour intended; honorific statues were no longer voted sparingly. Cf. Plut. *Ant.* 60. 2 f.; Dow, *HSCP* 67 (1963), 81 ff.; DS s.v. *statua*. Atticus' hostility to statues in honour of mere men is good epicurean doctrine; cf. Lucr. 3. 78; C. Bailey, *JRS* 41 (1951), 164). But honouring gods with statues was approved (Lucr. 6. 75).

counsel. Atticus' role does appear to have been genuinely disinterested. A rich and influential benefactor at this stage was a rare boon; 80,000 (or so it was said) Roman businessmen and their families were killed in Asia Minor at the end of 88; Mithridates' orders were executed eagerly by exploited Greeks.

3. 3. It . . . world. For such language cf. Aug. *RG* introduction and 13; Verg. *Aen.* 1. 230 f., 7. 258. The idea of Roman world-rule is first noticeable in Cicero, under Greek influence and when talking about Julius Caesar: Weinstock (1971), 52; cf. further note on 20. 5 (**prize**).

culture. With this contrast we might compare Verg. *Aen.* 6. 847 ff. with Petrochilos (1974), 141 ff. and Griffin (1985), 169 ff.

4. 1. Athens. N. has no word of the sieges or sack of Athens; the city fell to Sulla on 1 March 86. It seems likely that Atticus arrived shortly after. When Sulla returned after campaigning against Mithridates in 84, he collected and later carried off to Rome large quantities of statues, paintings, and books (including Aristotle's library). It seems unlikely that Atticus could do much to help; indeed he clearly profited by the rape, though this was apparently not held against him by the Athenians; cf. further Keaveney (1982), 124 f.; W. S. Ferguson, *Hellenistic Athens* (London 1911), 447 ff.; J. J. Pollitt, *Art of Rome* (Cambridge 1983), 63 f.; Plut. *Sulla*, 26.

captured. Cf. 8. 2 (**Marcus Brutus**) for Atticus' friendship across the generation barriers.

culture and learning. *Humanitas* (a term that encapsulates the virtues of a man: humane, educated, civilized) was a central element in Cicero's idealization of the 'circle' about the younger Scipio (Astin (1967), 302 ff.); not idealization alone, for to Cicero and Atticus there was a real human conduit of contact, Scaevola (see notes on 1. 4, **Torquatus** and 10. 3, **old age**), son-in-law of Laelius the Wise (Cic. *Am.* 1). Scaevola's legate Rutilius Cicero also knew, (Rawson (1975), 27 f.; Cic. *Rep.* 1. 13). Atticus' great friend Peducaeus (21. 4, **Lucius . . . him**) Cicero called an image of *humanitas* (*Fin.* 2. 58). N.'s characterization of Atticus here is markedly Ciceronian in tone ('you brought your name, your wisdom, your *humanitas* back from Athens': cf. *Sen.* 1; *Leg.* 2. 36, 3. 1). The idea and N.'s alleged preoccupation with it have attracted a good deal of cloudy speculation (but for some good sense cf. O. Nybakken, *TAPA* 70 (1939), 396 ff.); N. finds the characterization in Cicero (*supra*) and applies it sparingly (cf. 16. 1); 'that untranslatably Roman amalgam of kindness and culture, width of mind, and tact of manner' (SB i. 57).

so well. Cf. Petrochilos (1974), 24; Horsfall *EMC* 33 (1979), 85 f.; not all Roman compliments on Romans' ability to speak Greek well should be taken with equal seriousness, but there is no reason to suppose that Atticus was not quite exceptional.

so . . . acquired. For Atticus' qualities of voice and speech cf. note on 1. 3 (**extremely well**). *Suavitas*, which I have rendered as 'agreeable', was recognized by Cicero as an important quality in a friend (*Am.* 66). So too *lepos*, 'charm' or 'grace': compare Cicero's characterization of C. Iulius Caesar Strabo Vopiscus, aedile of 90 at *Tusc.* 5. 55 and *Brutus* 177 (*humanitas, suavitas, lepos*, etc.).

4. 2. Italy. As Augustus, on his way back from the East in 19, met Virgil at Athens; Virgil had intended to stay for three years but 'decided not to part from him and even to return (to Rome) with him' (*Vit. Don.* 35). Similarly the role of Horace, Virgil, Varius, and Plotius Tucca in Hor. *Serm.* 1. 5, in the train of Maecenas and Cocceius from Rome to Brundisium. Ancient travel was slow and often boring: great men might very reasonably welcome and seek out civilized travelling companions.

lead me. For Atticus' explanations of his non-participation in public affairs cf. 6. 1 (**waves of the sea**) and 10. 6–11. 1 (**but . . . remarkable**); at least here and in chapter 6, it looks very much as though N. is reporting one of Atticus' own explanations.

sense of duty. See note on 9. 4 (**services**): I translate 'officium'; 'mutual serviceableness between status-equals' (Crook (1967), 94; cf. ibid. 237). The services exchanged are in theory free, but are carefully weighed with the precisely appropriate degree of requital in view. Such calculated relationships are neither exclusively political, nor largely between patron and client, nor do they exclude what was called 'amicitia' ('friendship'). Cf. Gelzer (1969), 54 f., 66 f.; Ross Taylor (1964), 39 ff.; Wistrand (1978), 11 f., 27 f.; Brunt (1965), 4 = Seager (1969), 202; P. A. Brunt, *JRS* 76 (1986), 14 f. Atticus here balances his obligations, and Sulla approves his conclusions.

presents. Cf. note on 4. 5 (**consuls**); Sulla had his booty from Asia Minor and probably that from the sack of Athens in 86 to collect as well; 'presents' will not have been easy to define; yet no hint that N., or the Athenians, found Atticus blameworthy.

4. 3. head of a household. It is very curious that N. nowhere mentions Pilia, who married Atticus on 12 February 56 (perhaps not a first marriage if we think of Atticus' age). She was of an old family of Cora in southern Latium (Peilius, *CIL* i². 1509; R. Syme, *Augustan Aristocracy* (Oxford 1986), 314 n. 9), and probably the sister of Q. Pilius Celer (*Att.* 10. 1. 4 etc.). It was a happy marriage (*Att.* 8. 6. 4); she is often greeted by Cicero, and takes hard the unhappy marriage of her sister-in-law to Q. Cicero (see note on 5. 3, **match**; *Att.* 5. 11. 7). Had she not predeceased Atticus, she would presumably have been in N.'s list of those present at his death (21. 4). Cf. further note on 14. 3 (**income**) for his family estate.

placed . . . friends. Cf. note on 4. 2 (**sense of duty**). These 'urban duties' divide into private (you supply, e.g., news, money, defence in court) and public (you help, protect, and elevate the other person, in politics or in the courts, you recommend him and raise votes for him (cf. *Att.* 1. 4. 7 on Atticus and Quintus Cicero's election as plebeian aedile, 66 BC) and you contribute to showing him marks of public respect); Hellegouarc'h (1963), 152 ff. Atticus helps notably in Cicero's election as consul: SB i. 9 ff.; Ross Taylor (1964), 62 ff.; Nicolet (1980), 270 ff. Cf. note on *Att.* 5. 2 (**three-quarters**).

4. 4. exceptionally . . . Cicero. On the Nones of December 63 Atticus did lead the guard of knights posted by Cicero on the Capitol, when the senate debated what to do with the Catilinarian conspirators. In 58 Clodius, testified against by Cicero in 61, had ample revenge and in March Cicero went into exile; during the crisis, Atticus' advice was not all that it might have been, but characteristically (cf. note on 2. 3, **help**), his help when his friend was truly down and helpless was irreproachable (SB i. 14, 19 ff., 22; Rawson (1975), 113 ff.; no mention of the 250,000 HS in the letters). Atticus' role (if any) in Cicero's last perils remains impenetrably mysterious (cf. note on 9. 3, **Cicero**).

4. 5. consuls. This was in 65 BC; the form of dating by consuls had always been usual at Rome, but its employment was greatly facilitated by the publication of Atticus' own *liber annalis* (see note on 18. 1, **volume . . . order**). 'I think': few parts of the life have a firm chronological structure (see note on 7. 1, **Caesar's civil war**); here alone the absolute dating wavers, apparently because N. had never checked with Atticus. The *Latin Historians* was apparently not dedicated to Atticus (cf. p. 00), nor was the life of Atticus written obviously at its subject's request. Cicero, standing for consul, needed his friend's help, but it appears that in late 65 Atticus was in Epirus (*Att.* 1. 2. 2; SB i. 4 n. 3).

escorted. The departures and arrivals of distinguished men, officials, and, less obviously, private individuals, grew into formalized public occasions, when respect and regard might be displayed 'spontaneously'; cf. Weinstock (1971), 290; Nicolet (1980), 357; Griffin (1985), 61; T. E. V. Pearce, *CQ* 20 (1970), 313; S. MacCormack, *Hist.* 21 (1972), 721 ff.

5. 1. Quintus Caecilius. He died in 58 (see note on 5. 2, **three-quarters**). He was long remembered as a really hard money-lender (Sen. *Ep.* 118. 2). Cicero confirms (*Att.* 1. 12. 1; cf. 1. 1. 3) his professional ferocity and the disagreeable portrait given here. Atticus inherited Caecilius' house on the Quirinal (13. 2, **Tamphilus'**) and three-quarters of Caecilius' estate (5. 2, 14. 2); cf. Finley (1973), 53 f.

Lucius Lucullus. Valerius Maximus (7. 8. 5) relates that Caecilius owed both rank and fortune to Lucius Lucullus, probably (Cic. *Att.* 1. 1. 3) his partner in money-lending, and had always said that Lucullus would inherit; but Atticus did, and the Roman people dragged the money-lender's body about the streets at a rope's end. But if Caecilius had not been a knight, would his sister have married Atticus' well-born father? Valerius Maximus is often wrong: cf. Hopkins (1983), 241.

devotion. This translates *pietas* as at 17. 1: *pietas* towards his mother entailed for Atticus a similar feeling for her crabbed, greedy, and possibly unreliable brother. It paid off, and who was to call Atticus a legacy-hunter?

5. 2. three-quarters. The Latin is *ex dodrante*: proportions of an estate were treated as though fractions of an *as*, on a duodecimal basis; Bonner (1977), 181 ff. provides an introduction. Hideously difficult though this sounds, it had advantages, since interest was calculated monthly, i.e. likewise duodecimally. What is loosely called testamentary adoption (cf. Crook (1967), 112; A. Watson, *Law of Persons* (Oxford 1967), 87 f.) seems formally ruled out by the lawyers, but ten or so cases of something quite like it are found in the late republic (e.g. Cic. *Brut.* 212, *Off.* 3. 74, *Rab. Post.* 45). The most important and least clear 'parallel' is that of Caesar and Octavian (J. Crook, *CR* 4 (1954), 152 ff.; G. E. F. Chilver, *JRS* 44 (1954), 126 f.; S. Jameson, *Hist.* 24 (1975), 289). Atticus might now formally be called Q. Caecilius Q. f. Pomponianus Atticus, but often was not (Shackleton Bailey on 3. 22. 3); Cicero (*Att.* 3. 20. 1: 5 October 58) congratulates Atticus heartily, under his full name, on his uncle's

officium; Atticus' daughter was called Caecilia; and his freedmen
bore either name. See now also R. Syme, *Roman Papers*, iv (Oxford
1988), 159–74.

5. 3. match. Atticus' sister was roughly his contemporary (17. 1);
she had married Quintus Cicero before the writing of *Att.* 1. 5. 2.
Troubles had started already in 68, though they did not finally
divorce till 45–4, even if they came near in 50 (*Att.* 6. 2. 1–2). It
seems clear that Pomponia lacked her brother's tact and charm (*Att.*
5. 1. 4)! Cf. Hallett (1984), 171 f.

with Marcus. For Cicero's relations with Atticus SB i. 3 ff. is
masterly. Atticus was born in 110, Cicero in 106. They were friends
from their time as pupils. With whom? Shackleton Bailey, *Cicero*
(London 1971), 7 f. says at the house of Crassus. Cicero moved from
Crassus to Scaevola (cf. note on 1. 4, **Torquatus**), perhaps in March
90, when he was just over sixteen, and Atticus nearly twenty. It is
not certain that Atticus had also studied with Crassus (*Leg.* 1. 13 for
Atticus and Scaevola); in any case, Atticus was three and a half
years the elder (cf. SB i. 3), and Cicero is likelier to have 'caught up'
at the later stage, when the beginnings of close intellectual and social
relations are anyway perhaps more imaginable (cf. Rawson (1975),
13 ff.). Their friendship was probably, but not provably (cf. note on
9. 3, **Cicero**), interrupted only by death, nearly half a century later.

with Quintus. Gaston Boissier, *Cicero and his Friends* (Eng. tr.
London 1897), wears very well (235 ff.); cf. also Shackleton Bailey
Cicero, 67 ff.); the episode (see note on 7. 3, **as they were**) of the
Ciceros' pardon by Caesar shows Quintus in a most disagreeable
light.

ties of blood. Cf. 10. 2 'a man very like him' and note on 19. 2 (**he
... state**). N. lays stress upon the importance of shared tastes and
interests as a basis for friendship: cf. Cic. *Am.* 27, 28, 74, a text
dedicated to Atticus himself which N. had, I suggest (cf. p. 12 f),
studied with care. Common *studia* are fundamental to the theory and
practice of ancient friendship (Arist. *Eth. Nic.* 8. 2. 1; Cic. *Fam.*
5. 13. 5, 15. 2; Hor. *Serm.* 2. 6. 75; Macleod (1983), 283); Brunt
(1965), 1 ff. = Seager (1969), 199 ff.); N. turns wisely and
appropriately to Cicero's *De amicitia*.

5. 4. leading ... day. See the engrossing discussion by Ross Taylor
(1964), 98 ff.: Hortensius yielded the primacy when his defence of
Verres against Cicero failed. When thereafter they appeared on the

same side in court, Cicero delivered the peroration (ib. 116; on Hortensius as orator cf. Cic. *Brut.* 301 ff., 317 ff.; Kennedy (1972), 96 ff.).

renown. Hortensius 'at first made light of my consulship, but later, for twelve years, we acted most closely in important cases' (Cic. *Brut.* 313); cf. *Att.* 6. 6. 2 for a funeral tribute. For their relations in detail, cf. SB i. 7; Mitchell (1979), 173 f.

6. 1. optimates. Untranslatable; cf. Wistrand (1978), 32 f.; id. (1981), 8 f.; Syme (1939), 22; Ross Taylor (1964), 11 ff.; Hellegouarc'h (1963), 500 ff.; P. A. Brunt, *JRS* 58 (1968), 231 f. Not in any modern sense a 'party' (cf. note on 8. 4, **conspiratorial**). Though Atticus is not a senator, or a noble, he belongs; but it is above all aristocrats and the senate who are called *optimates* (more exclusive than *boni*). They uphold, even more than senatorial authority, their own privileges and traditional domination. They stand for 'cum dignitate otium', 'stability with *dignitas*' (defined in note on 2. 2, **standing**): cf. Wirszubski, *JRS* 44 (1954), 7 = Seager (1969), 189.

waves of the sea. An image with a very long history (Alcaeus, Theognis, Greek tragedy, Plato, Polybius); cf. Nisbet and Hubbard on Hor. *Carm.* 1. 14. Cf. further note on 10. 6 (**but . . . remarkable**) for its implications in N.'s day. Sallust uses similar language (*Jug.* 3. 1, notably 'hac tempestate') to condemn political ambitions. Of Atticus Cicero said 'Another and entirely justifiable way of thinking has led you to an honourable independence' (*Att.* 1. 17. 5; note Shackleton Bailey's translation of 'honestum otium' and cf. *Att.* 14. 20. 5). N. does not disguise the political weight that Atticus wields passively; there are only the briefest flickers of active involvement: cf. notes on 4. 3 (**placed . . . friends**) for 63 and 8. 1 (**when . . . Cassius**) with A. D. Momigliano, *JRS* 31 (1941), 152, for brief support of the assassins in 44. Neutrality was a virtue for knights (Syme (1939), 517); there were others besides Atticus (SB i. 5; notably also Momigliano, loc. cit. for Matius and Saufeius, for whom cf. note on 12. 3). For a man who took his *officia* and *amicitiae* seriously (see notes on 1. 4, **captivated**, and 4. 2, **sense of duty**), neutrality required courage and determination in the maintenance of a most delicate balance; cf. Jal (1963), 429 f. In 49 Caesar knew that Cicero was pulled strongly in both directions (*Att.* 9. 7a. 2). See further note on 7.3 inactivity.

6. 2. influence and standing. Cf. notes on *Cato*, 1. 3 (**aedile**) and *Att.* 21. 1 (**influence**) for the *gratia* and *dignitas* of Atticus.

traditional manner. Cf. *Cato*, 2. 2 (**law**), *Ages*. 4. 2, *Eum*. 8. 2 for similar mournful reflections about contemporary political morality. It is not clear that Atticus himself necessarily shared this disposition to trite moralizing.

involved. On bribery cf. Ross Taylor (1964), 67 f.; Shatzman (1975), 88 ff.; Gruen (1974), 218 ff., 271 ff. for details. Between 81 and 52 eight laws were passed to control it, and Atticus might have aspired, had he wished, to become praetor, even consul, just in the middle of that period. Again (cf. note on 6. 1, **waves of the sea**) the sequence of thought is very close to that in N.'s near contemporary Sallust (*Cat.* 3. 3: 'bribery and rapacity held sway . . . I took no part').

6. 3. public auction. Or only under exceptional circumstances (cf. 12. 3); a feature notably of the Sullan proscriptions and less successful under the triumvirs (Shatzman (1975), 40, 43; Syme (1939), 195). A definite, and understandable, prejudice existed against participation (cf. Sen. *Brev.* 12. 1). Auctioneers likewise attracted opprobrium: R. MacMullen, *Roman Social Relations* (New Haven 1974), 72, 140, etc. Cf. further Crook (1967), 219 f.

surety or a contractor. The *manceps* ('contractor') acts on behalf of a partnership of *publicani* to secure a public contract for (e.g.) road-works, army supplies, or tax-collecting. The *praes* stood surety for the fulfilment of the contract. Cf. Crook (1967), 244; *OCD*[2] s.v. *publicani, manceps*; E. Badian, (1972), 11 ff.

accused - jurisdiction. If there were more than one would-be prosecutor in a criminal case, a *divinatio* was held before the praetor to determine the principal accuser, as happened with Cicero and Caecilius before Glabrio before the trial of Verres opened (Ross Taylor (1964), 107). It was normal for there to be several secondary accusers (*subscriptores*) who might include those rejected in the *divinatio*: Gruen (1974), 323 f.; A. H. J. Greenidge, *Legal Procedure of Cicero's Time* (Oxford 1901), 465 f., 475 f. For prosecutions under the civil law cf. Crook (1967), 74 f. Only a rash man would have stood up to Atticus' *gratia* in court (cf. note on 21. 1, **influence**). Cf. J. M. Kelly, *Roman Litigation* (Oxford 1966), 31 ff. By disposition clearly Atticus, unlike Cato (see note on *Cato*, 2. 4, **republic**), was no habitual litigant. Lastly, a distinguished Roman such as Atticus might be requested to judge by the parties, or be proposed by the praetor in a civil suit: Crook (1967), 78 ff.; Greenidge, 265 ff.; Kelly, 102. Such activities took up a great deal of the younger Pliny's time (*Ep.* 1. 9. 2, 20. 12, 5. 1. 5, 6. 2. 7 with Sherwin-White's notes, and

Crook (1967), 34). But N. may mean, further, that Atticus also declined to serve (after 70 BC) on the panel of equestrian *iudices* for criminal trials.

6. 4. prefect. Prefects in this sense were knights appointed by (pro-) consuls or (pro-)praetors with or without specific functions; a procedure invaluable for lending authority to extortion or for motivating swift departures from Rome (Arnold (1914), 69; Hill (1952), 82 f.; Shackleton Bailey on *Att.* 5. 4. 3; 6. 2. 8). There appears (Nicolet i (1966), 436) no exact parallel for the purely honorary appointment described by N. here.

profit. Cicero says (*Fam.* 5. 20. 9) that he made 2. 2 million HS in Cilicia without breaking the law, 'salvis legibus' (Shatzman (1975), 413); he is eloquent to his brother (*QF* 1. 1. 8–9) on the temptations and dangers that Quintus will face. On the ways in which profits, often huge, and sometimes even licit, could be made cf. Shatzman (1975), 53–63, 69; cf. further notes on 6. 2 (**involved**) and 6. 5 (**served . . . crime**).

his staff. Quintus governed Asia for three years (like Verres in Sicily), 61–58; cf. Badian (1972), 80 f., SB *QF* 3. Cicero's first surviving letter to his brother on how to govern, is of engrossing interest. Legates were appointed by the senate on the governor's proposal and, if Atticus could have gone, clearly did not have to be senators. Cf. Arnold (1914), 67 f., with distrust, and B. Schleussner, *Die Legaten der römischen Republik* (Munich 1978).

6. 5. served . . . crime. He could, that is, have been a praetor had he (cf. 6. 1–2) wished for a senatorial career and exerted himself modestly: Gelzer (1969), 107; Wiseman (1971), 162 ff. Cf. Catull. 10. 9–13 for the portrait of a tight (or honest) governor; note on 6. 4 (**profit**); Cic. *Att.* 11. 1. 2; and Shatzman (1975), 60 for the consideration that Atticus could in fact have made a large licit profit. The existence of a permanent extortion court (*quaestio de rebus repetundis*: cf. E. Badian, *OCD²* s.v. *repetundae*) is sufficient evidence for the scale of the problem; see too Ross Taylor (1964), 98 ff. for a fine introduction to the role a successful prosecution could play in a political career.

sense of duty. For *officium* see note on 4. 2. For prosecutions cf. the table at Shatzman (1975), 106. The sums involved were huge: Frank, *ESAR* i. 298; Plut. *Mar.* 34 for a startling example. Cicero claimed Verres made 40 million HS in Sicily, but other figures are quoted (Shatzman (1975), 436). N. refers to (unsalaried) posts in provincial administration as a perfectly normal source of income (cf. previous note). The notion of such licit profit has become curiously shocking; cf. rather William Hickey's *Journals* on life in eighteenth-century Bengal.

7. 1. Caesar's civil war. 7. 1–11. 4 is the only section of the life organized on a clear chronological basis (cf. pp. 9–10); N. knows Atticus was born in 110 (21. 1), though he gives no exact date as he does for his death (22. 3). Here the approximate age is in keeping with the generally loose temporal structure N. prefers. Caesar crossed the Rubicon on 11 January 49.

age. Fifty brought exemption from military service, sixty from jury service, and, after Augustus, from attendance in the Senate (Balsdon (1969), 169). Note *Pet. Cons.* 9 of Catiline's equestrian brother-in-law, inactive both by disposition and years! Cf. Powell on Cic. *Sen.* 34.

own fortune. To lend financial aid to a friend in need was to perform what was due to a friend and would not be construed by Caesar as a hostile act: SB i. 37; Brunt (1965), 10 f. = Seager (1969), 208 f.; Wistrand (1978), 45; Jal (1963) 429 ff. Atticus' masterly perception of the ethical bases and political realities of a neutral position dominates these chapters (cf. note on 6. 1, **waves of the sea**).

close. This translates 'coniunctum'; the word can also denote kinship and a link has been sought—unconvincingly—through Pompey's fifth wife, of the Caecilii Metelli by adoption, and hence through uncle Caecilius. The word as easily suggests friendship (for example Atticus and Brutus, Cic. *Brut.* 10; cf. note on 8. 2, **adviser**); though Pompey and Atticus had long been acquainted (*Att.* 2. 17. 3, 3. 13. 1, 4. 9. 1), they were not close (SB i. 7). For the uncertainties of Cicero and Atticus in 49 cf. SB i. 42 ff.; M. Wistrand, *Cicero Imperator* (Göteborg 1979), 61 ff.; Rawson (1975), 188 ff.; Brunt *JRS* 76 (1986), 12 ff.

7. 2. through him. Pompey in 49 had a very large *clientela* (Syme (1939), 30 ff.; id., *JRS* 28 (1938), 113 ff. for the fascinating case of Labienus) and many also followed him out of personal loyalty (cf. Jal (1963), 430; Brunt (1965), 19 = Seager (1969), 217; Brunt, *JRS* 76, 26 ff.; see above all Plut. *Pomp.* 61. 4).

offence. Atticus' decision not to support Pompey actively was resented deeply by some, though (7. 1) not by Pompey: *Att.* 11. 6. 2; SB i. 33; Brunt, *JRS* 76 (1986), 15, 22. Cicero eventually went, unhappily (cf. note on 7. 3, **as they were**, and Wistrand (1978), 39 ff.). Pompey declared that he would regard those who did not follow him and those who did follow Caesar on a par (Caes. *BC* 1. 33. 2; Wistrand (1978), 43).

7. 3. inactivity. Like N.'s repeated use of the storm image as an argument for inactivity (cf. notes on 6. 1, **waves of the sea** and 10. 6. But it is likely (M. Griffin, *G&R* 33 (1986), 76 n. 6; cf. e.g. Lucr. 1. 31, 3. 18) that language and attitude are in part recognizably Epicurean. N. never mentions Epicureanism by name and shows no particular sympathy, yet he appears to retail authentic Epicurean language and thought, and may here reflect Atticus' views in Atticus' language. Cf. further p. 13.

by letter. To pay and to punish: cf. Dio 42. 50. 2 f.; (Caes.) *Bell. Afr.* 64. 2. Others were fined or 'invited' to lend money; opponents who had been killed, or had not been pardoned, had their property auctioned. Antony bought Pompey's palace and coveted Varro's estate (Shatzman (1975), 352 ff.; Rice Holmes, 3. 234 f.; M. Gelzer, *Caesar* (Eng. tr. Oxford 1968), 262; N. M. Horsfall, *BICS* 19 (1972), 121).

as they were. Cicero, Quintus (they were in the middle of a furious row) and Atticus' nephew the younger Quintus were pardoned in mid-July 47; N. here attributes to Atticus a role that does not appear in Cicero's letters to him (cf. *Att.* 11. 21. 3, 22. 1); cf. SB i. 45 ff.; Rawson (1975), 205 ff.

8. 1. when . . . Cassius. N. refers to a transient moment, just after the Ides and hardly noticed by historians: Atticus exclaimed that the cause was lost if Caesar was given a public funeral (*Att.* 14. 10. 1), defended Brutus and Cassius as though Cicero were attacking them (ib. 14. 14. 2), but within a fortnight (ib. 14. 20. 5) was talking about Epicurus and abstention! Cf. A. D. Momigliano, *JRS* 31 (1941), 153; some Caesarians had become alarmed and made wills in Cicero's favour by way of insurance (*Att.* 14. 3. 2, 14. 5; Wistrand (1981), 37 n. 81). N. refers to 'the Bruti': Atticus' friend Marcus (see next note) and Decimus (see note on 9. 1, **Modena**).

8. 2. Marcus Brutus. He was one of Atticus' last friends among the grand nobility; a relationship of which N. makes much (9. 3, 10. 1,

16. 1, 18. 3); cf. SB i. 53; Cic. *Brutus*, 10 and ed. Douglas, p. xviii. Brutus was born about 85; Atticus was thus 25 years his senior, as he had been (cf. note on 4. 1, **captured**) 28 years Sulla's junior.

adviser. Brutus had long known Cicero, who found him disapproving (*Att.* 14. 20. 5); Atticus, long a friend (ib. 5. 21. 10), urged closer acquaintance (ib. 6. 1. 3). The *Brutus*, written in 46 as a dialogue between Cicero, Atticus, and Brutus, does not reflect a specially affectionate triumvirate. What was Atticus to advise in 44? He asked Cicero (*Att.* 14. 20. 4)! Cf. SB i. 52 f.

Daily companion. 'Convictus' can refer in general to 'life together' but often refers more narrowly to regular meetings across the dinner-table; cf. Hor. *Serm.* 1. 4. 96, 6. 47; P. White, *JRS* 68 (1978), 80 n. 20; Aug. *Ep.* fr. 37 Malc. (to Horace).

8. 3. some . . . knights. The only sure reference to this project; the references in Cicero *Ep. ad Brut.* 12/14. 4 and 17/26. 3 are in arguably spurious documents. Cf. SB i. 53; Syme (1939), 102.

Gaius Flavius. Called 'a financier' by Syme (loc. cit.), he is a shadowy figure (Nicolet, ii (1974), 880; SB *Fam.* ii. 451 f.); he was a friend of Brutus and, as an aide-de-camp of his, died at Philippi.

8. 4. taking sides. A situation more difficult than in 49 only in that Atticus is a close friend of Brutus; he contrives therefore to help the man, not the cause (8. 6); cf. note on 7. 1 (**age**) for 49 and 2. 3 (**Athens**) for helping his schoolfriend the young Marius. N. repeatedly in these chapters presents a preference for personal over factional loyalties as being the essence of Atticus' policy; cf. 9. 5.

scheme. Here, and at (e.g.) 4. 2, 6. 4, 17. 1, 21. 5, 22. 2, one may wonder whether N. preserves some, or much, of Atticus' own outlook and language; cf. note on 7. 3, (**inactivity**) for Epicurean terminology.

conspiratorial association. This translates 'consensionis globus': *consensio* can carry either good or bad implications (Hellegouarc'h (1963), 125); *globus* is exceptionally rare in political language (cf. Sall. *Jug.* 85. 10). Throughout this commentary I am careful to avoid the word 'party'; it might be used justifiably of *optimates* and *populares* (cf. note on 6. 1, **optimates**), were it realized that 'party' had little or nothing of its modern value (cf. P. A. Brunt, *JRS* 58 (1968),

230 ff.). N. here talks of a temporary association; Brutus does not have any sort of 'party': cf. M. I. Finley, *Politics in the Ancient World* (Cambridge 1983), 97 ff.; R. Seager, *JRS* 62 (1972), 53 ff.; Syme (1939), 11.

dissent. Note the power exercised by the skilled non-participator. Only at 9. 7 does N. let it appear that Atticus' course of inaction was not approved. If Atticus was a 'political animal' (Shackleton Bailey's translation at *Att.* 4. 6. 1, cf. 2. 12. 4, 12. 23. 2; cf. also Nicolet, i (1966), 709; id. ii (1974), 990), he preferred the security of his burrow.

8. 5. exile. The Senate decreed (5 June) that Brutus and Cassius (last seen at 8. 1) would by and by be assigned provinces; for the moment Brutus was to supervise the corn trade from Sicily, Cassius that from Asia. This was clearly insulting (cf. *Att.* 15. 9. 1; App. *Civ.* 3. 18, 20). The next month Crete was assigned to Brutus, Cyrene to Cassius. In August Brutus left Italy and eventually seized Macedonia, as did Cassius Syria. Cf. RH, *ARE* i. 17, 196 f.; *MRR* ii. 321.

8. 6. in desperate straits. Cf. 2. 2, 4. 4, 7. 1, 9. 3, 11. 1 for the recurrent motif of Atticus helping his friends in their darkest hours. Cf. Plut. *Sulla*, 10.

in despair. Brutus fled from Italy in August 44, and spent the autumn in Athens, studying philosophy and preparing for war. For his victorious campaign in Epirus against C. Antonius brother of Mark Antony in early 43 cf. RH, *ARE* i. 45; Plut. *Brut.* 25–6; M. L. Clarke, *The Noblest Roman* (London 1981), 51. As for the size of the 'sums involved, we might remember that the minimum estate of a knight, or the cost of about 330 acres of unimproved Italian land, or of a prime stallion, was 400,000 HS. For the ample and contemporary material in Varro's *Res rusticae* cf. Frank, *ESAR* i. 363 ff.

9. 1. Modena. See Rawson (1975), 278 ff.; RH, *ARE* i. 34 ff., 194. Decimus Brutus occupied Mutina, ignoring Antony's instructions to him to leave Cisalpine Gaul, which he now claimed as his province. Antony besieged the ex-conspirator and Octavian marched to relieve him. The Senate sent an embassy requesting Antony to withdraw; Octavian was joined by the consul Hirtius, then by his colleague Pansa. Antony was heavily defeated on 14 and 21 (?) April, but Pansa was fatally wounded in the first battle, and Hirtius killed in the second. On the 22nd Antony raised the siege.

character of a seer. This renders 'divinatio': but I am not convinced, and wonder whether N. is here using the word in the sense of 'divinitas', 'godlike character'. Cf. note on 16. 4 (**that . . . use**).

9. 2. left Italy. Antony left Rome on 28 November 44 and made for Cisalpine Gaul (i.e. left Italy, as legally defined), though the motion declaring him a public enemy was not for now put to the vote (Cic. *Phil.* 3. 20; Syme (1939), 126; RH, *ARE* i. 33; H. Frisch, *Cicero's Fight for the Republic* (Copenhagen 1946), 152 f. A. *tumultus* (cf. note on 2. 2, **Cinna**) was probably declared on 2 February 43 (Lintott (1968), 154), and Antony was finally declared an enemy of Rome (*hostis*) the day after the second battle of Mutina (22 April: Vell. 2. 64. 3; Lintott (1968), 155).

his wife. Fulvia, wife of Clodius, Curio, and then Antony, was living at Calenus' house (Cic. *Phil.* 12. 18); her life was not easy (App. *Civ.* 3. 51), but no other account of the situation quite parallels N.'s. Fulvia has attracted a lurid press: cf. Balsdon (1962), 49 f.; J. P. Hallett, *AJAH* 2 (1977), 151 ff. But she was no innocent victim of ungallant and brutal persecution: she had clearly been active alongside Antony in the wholesale corruption of the summer of 44; note particularly her support for Deiotarus of Galatia (RH, *ARE* i. 5 f.; Shackleton Bailey, *Philol.* 126 (1982), 221; Cic. *Att.* 14. 12. 1; id. *Phil.* 2. 93, 95). Cf. further the note on 9. 5 (**bought . . . date**).

9. 3. Cicero. The last letter surviving is of November 44; Cicero was killed on 7 December 43. It is simply not known why the correspondence ends where it does: an accident of transmission, perhaps, or disapproval of Cicero's fight against Antony (cf. next note and 9. 7, **criticized**). Cicero may likewise have disapproved of Atticus' stand. There is no word in N. of Cicero's death; Atticus saves (10. 5) his dearest friend Kanus from the proscriptions, not Cicero. Cf. SB i. 56.

outraging Antony. Cf. SB i. 54 f. For all his friendship with the absent Brutus, Atticus was not enthusiastic about a stand against Antony. In late May 44 Cicero urges Atticus to think hard about his position (*Att.* 15. 8); on 25 October (ib. 15. 13. 1) Cicero writes: 'I agree with you that I ought neither to lead the van nor to bring up the rear'; a page later: 'you say you know nothing about Brutus'; cf. ib. 16. 14. 1.

short of. Cf. note on 2. 3 (**help**); Syme (1939), 174 f.; RH, *ARE* i.
54 ff. for hostility to Antony, his family, and supporters. Again (cf. p.
12 n. 24), apparently only N. attests the flight of Antonians from
Rome; Atticus' support of fugitives is after all a leitmotiv of the life.

9. 4. Volumnius. This was a singularly wise act of generosity (cf.
10. 2, 12. 4); that is not to suggest that all Atticus' acts of kindness
were necessarily calculating, but it is rarely quite so clear that, given
that they occur within a system resting upon exchange of *officia* (cf.
note on 4. 2, **sense of duty**), they were also sound investments.
Atticus' friend was (cf. note on 12. 4, **aide-de-camp**) *praefectus
fabrum*, that is, at this date, not chief engineer but aide-de-camp
(Suolahti (1955), 205 ff.) to Antony; thus perhaps the same man as
the P. Volumnius Eutrapelus to whom Cicero writes *Fam.* 7. 32, 33:
a friend of Antony's at whose house Cicero once met Antony's
mistress Cytheris (*Fam.* 9. 26; hilarious). He was mentioned by
Horace (*Ep.* 1. 18. 31) and was possibly a minor poet (Schanz–
Hosius, i. 315). But the identification of Atticus' friend, Cicero's
friend, and the poet as one person is not certain (Shackleton Bailey
on *Att.* 15. 8. 1).

great fears. Cf. notes on 9. 2 (**his wife**) and 9. 5 (**bought . . . date**)
for the persecution of Fulvia.

services. Cf. note on 4. 3 (**placed**) for the range of services that
officia can cover; Antony (10. 4) remembers Atticus' *officia* to Fulvia
and again (cf. notes on 10. 4, **remembered** and 11. 1, **he could**)
kindness is shown to pay off.

surety. Bail, in civil law, can be secured either through a promise to
pay, or through a guarantee by another person that you will appear
(so Hor. *Serm.* 1. 1. 11; 1. 9. 36, 75). See Crook (1967), 75 f.; A.
Berger, *Enc. Dict. Rom. Law* (Philadelphia 1963), s.v. *vadimonium*,
sponsor.

9. 5. bought . . . date. Cf. note on 10. 4 (**remembered**) for Fulvia's
use of Caesar's papers to enrich herself; it is easy to imagine her
enemies' glee in Antony's absence. But she was to be just as greedy
again in the proscriptions (App. *BC* 4. 29; Dio 47. 8. 2, 4). Payment
by a fixed date was a common procedure, copiously illustrated by
the tablets of the financier Jucundus from Pompeii (Crook (1967),
220; J. Andreau, *Les Affaires de M. Jucundus* (Rome 1974), 99 ff.; see
also Hor. *Epod.* 2. 69).

stepped . . . terms. Fulvia was clearly at this date thought a bad risk, as the cy of Athens had been (see note on 2. 4, **when . . . terms**); the same verb 'interposuit' is used here, which suggests the same procedure; the loans were not, that is, really interest-free (though that could happen; Plut. *Cat. min.* 6. 4; Shatzman (1975), 78), but Atticus passed on the favourable rates that he could himself obtain (6 per cent as it might be, cf. Cic. *Fam.* 5. 6. 2 (62 BC); Finley (1973), 53 f.; Frank, *ESAR* i. 352 f.). Atticus took a small but generous risk; only the alert reader, who recognizes the force of 'interposuit', will perceive, however, that Atticus loses nothing and wins, it turns out, invaluable goodwill.

people. Cf. 8. 4 (**taking sides**).

9. 7. criticized. Cicero may have been among the critics (cf. note on 9. 3, **Cicero**; SB i. 56). Material critical of Atticus could have been found (SB i. 29, 72), but its inclusion would not have been consonant with N.'s essentially panegyrical approach (cf. p. 10). Chapter 15 does hint at what some will have found a difficult side of Atticus' character.

'bad' citizens. 'mali' is clearly language used by *optimates* of their opponents (more often in the singular). See Wirszubski, *JRS* 45 (1955), 6 f. = Seager (1969), 188 f.; Ross Taylor (1964), 11 ff.; Hellegouarc'h (1963), 526 ff.

commend. Though N. is notably concerned to report the favourable impression that Atticus gave to so many (see note on 3. 1, **seem**).

10. 1. to Italy. After a three-day meeting to establish themselves as 'triumvirs for establishing the republic' near Bologna in Cisalpine Gaul in late October Octavian, Antony, and Lepidus moved south into Italy proper (cf. 9. 2), and reached Rome in late November; Cicero was (cf. note on 10. 4, **proscribe**) murdered on 7 December. See Dio. 47. 1–2; App. *BC* 4. 1–7; RH, *ARE* i. 68 ff.

Cicero. Not a word of Cicero's death; cf. note on 9. 3 (**Cicero**) for Atticus' relations with him in the last months and p. xvi. for N. on Cicero. Had Atticus tried to save his friend, N. would have said so, but the realist Atticus could hardly have tried after Cicero delivered the *Philippics*. Nor indeed (cf. 10. 5, 12. 2) did he thereafter distance himself from those responsible for Cicero's death.

10. 2. shortly before. Startling vicissitudes of fortune are a conventional element in writing about the civil wars (Hor. *Carm.* 2. 1. 3 with the notes of Nisbet and Hubbard; App. *BC* 4. 13; Jal (1963), 351). The meeting near Bologna (cf. note on 10. 1, **to Italy**) included discussion of the proscriptions to be held; the lists were put up on the night of 27–8 November, so Atticus was in no special hurry. The antiquarian Varro's friends competed to hide him (App. *BC* 4. 47; Horsfall *BICS* 19 (1972), 124 f.); Valerius Maximus lists *exempla* of those hidden by their slaves (6. 8. 5, 6, 7).

very like him. Cf. *Att.* 13. 31. 4, 41. 1 (a possible marriage between Cicero's nephew Quintus and Canus' daughter?), 15. 21. 2. He should perhaps be called correctly Kanus. This friend of Atticus is an apparently obscure figure who may have tempted the proscribers by his quietly acquired wealth. But he was perhaps the brother of L. Gellius Poplicola, *cos.* 72, and therefore the elder of the two brothers in Catul. 74, 80, 88, 89; see Shackleton Bailey on *Att.* 4. 3. 2.

10. 3. goodness. 'bonitas' is a favourite word (cf. 9. 1, 21. 1; *Milt.* 8. 3; *Tim.* 5. 1), rare before Cicero, who used it heavily.

old age. Cf. 1. 4 (**captivated**) and 5. 3 on the length of Atticus' friendships. This was a recurring motif also in Cic. *Am.* (33, 74: difficult to retain early friends, because relations are based on immature tastes. But Atticus did; cf. p. 12 for links of the life with Cicero's *De Amicitia*). We have seen that Atticus' great capacity for friendship is a central theme of N.'s work (see notes on 1. 4, **captivated** and 5. 3, **ties of blood**). Though it is unwise to make much of Cicero's contacts with survivors of the 'Scipionic Circle' (Rawson (1975), 14), it is pleasant to recall that Laelius the Wise, 'foremost in the renown of his friendships' (Cic. *Am.* 5), was the leading speaker of Cicero's dialogue on friendship; Atticus was the dedicatee, and both had been pupils (cf. notes on 1. 4, **Torquatus** and 4. 1, **captured**) of Laelius' son-in-law Scaevola. Atticus, says Cicero, will recognize himself in Laelius (5; cf. Brunt (1965), 6 = Seager (1969), 204). It is no accident that N. echoes the dialogue so often: cf. p. 12.

10. 4. proscribe them. Cicero delivered the first *Philippic* on 1 September 44; his execution was to be a leading item in the proscriptions agreed on near Bologna (see note on 10. 1, **to Italy**). His brother and nephew were also killed, but there appears to be no other evidence for Antony's systematic persecution of his followers and friends. Cf. Rawson (1975), 271 ff., 283; RH, *ARE*, i. 23 ff.; Syme (1939), 191.

remembered . . . at once. Atticus had taken out insurance, by helping both Fulvia (9. 4 ff.) and Brutus' mother (11. 4); it worked, so he manages to save Kanus' life and also Saufeius' property (12. 4). Stories of escape, and of those who at their peril assist escapers are common; it is Antony's conduct here that is exceptional (though cf. App. *BC* 4. 45; Dio 47. 7. 5, 8. 5; Wistrand, *Laud. Turiae*, 24 f., 44 f.) Cf. Syme (1939), 192; RH, *ARE* i. 72 ff. The autograph letter is a fine touch: it was treated as a sign of respect and affection, and as particularly pleasant to receive: A. B. Miller, *Roman Etiquette of the Late Republic* (Lancaster, Pa. 1914), 61 f.

the proscribed. The figures (Syme (1939), 191 n. 3) are confused; App. *BC* 4. 5 says that 300 senators and 2000 knights were decided on at the Bologna meeting; there was also (4. 6) a priority list of 12 or 17 names (including Cicero). The first lists, on whitened boards, were put up during the night of 27 November 43; cf. App. *BC* 4. 7, Dio 47. 3. 2. Those who helped the proscribed were likewise to be killed (Dio 47. 8. 1).

10. 5. guard. Cf. Dio 47. 10. 4, 12. 1, 13. 1; App. *BC* 4. 15 'some too perished quite apart from the triumvirs' intent, from ignorance or through plotting.'

10. 6. But . . . remarkable. Cf. 6. 1 (**waves of the sea**). M. Griffin, *G&R* 33 (1986), 76 n. 6 notes a similarity with the language of Lucr. 2. 1–2 and Cic. *Rep*. 1. 1 (a view introduced disparagingly), but it is not distinctively Epicurean (Cic. *TD* 5. 5, *Off*. 3. 2); however, given that N. does appear elsewhere to echo Atticus' use of that school's language (see note on 7. 3, **inactivity**), the suggestion that he may be doing so here too, if less distinctively, is attractive. There are Epicureans who support Caesar, who are neutral, and who oppose the dictator energetically (A. D. Momigliano, *JRS* 31 (1941), 152 f.; Nicolet i. (1966), 708 ff.). The position of Atticus' dear friend Saufeius is (cf. 12. 3) uncertain, as is (see note on 17. 3, **philosophers**) the strength of Atticus' own Epicureanism. His beliefs may therefore not be a relevant factor when considering his neutrality. Likewise, his friends, as we have come to expect, are of the most varied political loyalties; his ambiguities, or indecision (SB i. 51 ff.) remain impenetrable.

11. 1. emerged. This word carries the storm image over into the next section.

he could. It is easy to misinterpret Atticus' apparent altruism, since we are unused to thinking of a society whose wheels are oiled by *officia* and *beneficia* (see notes on 4. 2, **sense of duty** and 11. 5, **grateful**); Cic. *De officiis* and Sen. *De beneficiis* discuss the issues very fully. That is not to suggest that Atticus never acted without hope of return. But the system also worked in Atticus' favour: cf. notes on 10. 2, (**shortly before**) and 10. 4 (**remembered**) for Fulvia and Volumnius, 7. 2 (**through him**) for the legacies he received and 22. 4 (**men of substance**) for the size of his funeral procession.

rewards. These were offered both to informers and to the actual killers. The text Appian (*BC* 4. 8) gives of the proclamation is not necessarily authentic (Syme (1939), 190 n. 1); cf. RH, *ARE* i. 72 f. for a summary of the terms.

Epirus. On the route that Cicero (Plut. *Cic.* 47) thought of taking to join Brutus in Macedonia; the alternatives were to flee to Sextus Pompeius in Sicily, or to Cornificius in North Africa. For the refugees in Epirus cf. Dio 47. 12. 1, App. *Civ.* 4. 36. See Syme (1939), 192.

11. 2. After ... Brutus. In the first battle of Philippi (23 October 42) Brutus crushed Octavian and Antony Cassius, who committed suicide shortly after: Clarke, *The Noblest Roman*, 68 f.; RH, *ARE* i. 85 f.; Syme (1939), 205. The second battle took place three weeks later: RH, *ARE* i. 85 ff.; Clarke, *The Noblest Roman*, 70 f. Brutus was defeated and sought death shortly after: cf. notably Plut. *Brut.* 51–2.

L. Iulius Mocilla. A mystery of sorts; Mocilla looks, as presented, to be a significant figure, but is quite unknown elsewhere. It is possible that the MSS of N. have garbled the name of L. Tillius Cimber (his name is often garbled). He was active in the conspiracy against Caesar and (App. *BC* 4. 102, 105) served Brutus in northeast Greece.

A. Torquatus. Problematic: we may leave aside his relative Lucius (see note on 1. 4, **Torquatus**). Apart from the present passage, N. refers also to an A. Torquatus at 15. 3 whose business affairs Atticus manages: not necessarily the man mentioned here. An A. Torquatus was praetor in 70 BC, fled to Athens in 46–5 (and there received Cicero, *Fam.* 6. 1–4), and is thanked by Cicero at *Fin.* 2. 72 for help when he was himself in exile. Also to be borne in mind are the quaestor of 43 BC (under Pansa, *MRR* ii. 341) and the Torquatus mentioned in Hor. *Ep.* 1. 5. 3 and *Carm.* 4. 7. 23. J. F. Mitchell (*Hist.* 15 (1966), 23 ff.) thinks (p. 26) that N. here refers to the quaestor of

43 who is also the person known to Horace, while Shackleton Bailey (on *Att.* 5. 1. 5, *Fam.* 6. 1. 1) considers the praetor of 70 to be the man mentioned here. It is this passage that is at the heart of the difficulty: Horace's ex-quaestor friend may be the son of the Torquatus of 1. 4 (Mitchell). Shackleton Bailey's identification does have considerable plausibility, in that Atticus would here be helping an elderly aristocrat, a friend of Cicero's, a near-contemporary, who had followed Pompey in 49 and was now, logically, following Brutus.

to Samothrace. Exiles on Samothrace are not attested elsewhere, though we know of followers of Brutus who fled to Thasos and shortly surrendered to Antony on his way to Athens: App. *BC* 4. 136; RH, *ARE* i. 89.

11. 3. It . . . calculation. For reluctance to enter into details cf. *Praef.* 8, with notes; in passages such as this we need to remember that Greek panegyric does appear to have influenced N.: we must suspend our reluctance to agree that it is morally advantageous to us to read the praises of good men. Cf. note on 19. 1 (**actual examples**) on the exemplary character of this life.

11. 4. prospered. Fulvia he helped in adversity (5. 4), though he had not flattered Antony in prosperity (8. 5); Servilia's son was a dear friend (8. 2, 9. 3), and in the spring of 44 (cf. note on 8. 1, **when . . . Crassus**) Atticus lent him a little active support (SB i. 52 f.; *Att.* 15. 11. 2, 17. 2). Servilia, his mother, was a *chère amie* of Julius Caesar, a half-sister of Cato, and a great power in republican circles (Clarke, *The Noblest Roman*, 11; Balsdon (1962), 51 f.; SB i. 7).

11. 5. He . . . avenge. 'Inimicitiae', 'feuds'; 'iniuria', 'injury'. Political conflict did not normally make for personal hostility in republican Rome; unjust, unfair, extreme action had to be taken before actual enmity developed, durable (indeed heritable), and dangerous: see Brunt (1965), 13, 19 = Seager (1969), 211, 217; Hellegouarc'h (1963), 166 f.; Jal (1963), 37, 429. Forgiveness is a favourite theme of contemporary ethics (Hor. *Ep.* 2. 2. 210, 1. 7. 69, etc.; see note on 17. 3, **life**).

grateful. 'Do not keep mentioning your *officia*; the recipient should remember them'. (Cic. *Am.* 71; cf. Sen. *Ben.* 2. 10. 4, 11; also Cic. *Leg.* 1. 32, *Off.* 3. 25; Wistrand (1978), 10 f.

11. 6. each . . . fortune. Cited again at 19. 1, and at Cic. *Parad.* 5. 34; a line from an unidentified comic poet, printed as fr. xix of the uncertain lines of uncertain poets in Ribbeck's collection of Roman comic fragments, *Scaenicorum Romanorum poesis fragmenta*, ii³ (Leipzig 1898), 125. Stray echoes of Roman comedy are part of the common theatrical culture of Cicero's generation; cf. Griffin (1985), 200 f. The original of the Latin might be from the comic poet Philemon, because of an echo at Plaut. *Trin.* 363; F. Stoessl, *RhM* 122 (1979), 22.

himself. We are here at the heart of Latin proverbial wisdom: Appius Claudius the Blind, consul in 307 and 296 was said to have said in his *carmen* ('poem'—whatever that was: see Gratwick, *CHCL* ii. 138 f.) that each man was the smith (*faber*) of his own fortune (Ps. Sall. *Ep. ad Caes*. 1. 2); so too Sen. *Ep.* 36. 5 'fortune has no rights over our *mores*'; Ter. *Ad.* 399; Liv. 24. 14. 7. See A. Otto's invaluable collection of Latin proverbs *Die Sprichwörter der Römer* (repr. Hildesheim 1965), 143 f.

12. 1. Marcus Vipsanius Agrippa. Cf. M. Reinhold, *Marcus Agrippa* (Geneva, NY 1933). Agrippa was probably born in 64 (conventionally in 63); Octavian's indispensable general, but no unlettered soldier, unimaginable as a friend of Atticus except on grounds of time-serving! He had studied with Octavian in Greece (Suet. *Aug.* 8. 2), prosecuted Cassius in 43, was interested in declamation (Sen. *Contr.* 2. 4. 12 f.), believed strongly in making public all works of art (Plin. *NH* 35. 26), and undertook huge public works at Rome for the general benefit as early as 34. On the marriage cf. further notes on 19. 4 (**as a girl** and **Drusilla**).

Caesar's power. N.'s language preserves some of the earliest ideological evaluations of the young Octavian; cf. notes on 19. 3 (**hitherto**) and 20. 5 (**prizes** and **of the world**). 'Power' (*potentia*) is a word N. does not necessarily use with an implied condemnation of absolute power (cf. *Paus.* 3. 5, *Dion* 9. 5), though he could do so (see note on *Cat.* 2. 2, **office**). On Agrippa's own *gratia* cf. note on 12. 2 (**money**).

he ... particular. The engagement probably took place in 37 (but see note on 12. 2, **marriage**). After he had spared Atticus' life in 43 (10. 4, **remembered**), Antony was presumably in a strong position to influence the betrothal, which would serve to cement and even finance the accord reached between himself and Octavian at Brundisium in 40. The exact political motive for the engagement— and we must suppose that the element of pragmatic calculation was strong—is not easily definable.

aristocratic. *Generosus* is perhaps not as strong as *nobilis* (Cic. *Parad.* 3. 20, but see Gelzer (1969), 38). Cf. *Dion* 1. 2, Cic. *S. Rosc.* 15, Sall. *BJ* 85. 15, Liv 4. 55. 3, and Hor. *Carm.* 3. 1. 10 where being *generosus* is thought of as a relevant factor in elections. N. avoids the highly controversial technical language of nobility (P. A. Brunt, *JRS* 72 (1982), 1 ff.).

12. 2. It . . . republic. 20. 4 confirms Atticus' good relations with Antony (cf. note at 20. 4, **no loss**). The goodwill suggested by the pact of Brundisium (cf. note at 20. 4, **lands**) was transitory. Lepidus was expelled from the triumvirate in 36 and relations between the two surviving partners declined swiftly (Syme (1939), 259 ff.). By the time of Atticus' death in 32 he may already have been formally a *hostis* of Rome (so Suet. *Aug.* 17. 2, doubtfully). Until Antony's death in 30, and indeed beyond, to speak well of him required courage. 'This is not to be concealed' clearly suggests composition at a time when anti-Antonian feeling was already running high.

marriage. Atticus' daughter Caecilia was on the conventional view born in 51, after Cicero went to Cilicia, and betrothed in 37 (cf. note on 19. 4, **Drusilla**). M. Reinhold (*CPh* 67 (1972), 119 ff.) suggests 56–5, early in Atticus' marriage to (see note on 4. 3, **head of a household**) Pilia, with a betrothal to Agrippa during some moment of peace in 43–2. Cicero and Atticus were both clearly delighted with the frisky toddler in their lives ('hilaritas' is a favourite word). Even if she was born in 51, she can be writing letters to her father five years later (so Cic. *Att.* 12. 1. 1)! Were she born in 56–5, the complete silence about her in the letters of book 4 would be hard to explain; likewise the fact that in September 51 Cicero had still never seen her (*Att.* 5. 19. 2). Could her family really have stayed uninterruptedly in Epirus that long? She became a pupil of the distinguished teacher Q. Caecilius Epirota, Atticus' freedman, who was sacked on suspicion of undue familiarity towards her (Suet. *Gramm.* 16). Cf. Syme, *The Augustan Aristocracy* (1986), 314.

money. The proscriptions of 43–2 were not a financial success (cf. note on 6. 3, **public auction**); on a saturated market Atticus could clearly have made colossal profits.

dangers and inconveniences. Cf. Atticus' help as a constant motif of these chapters: 7. 3; 10. 4; 11. 2; 12. 3, 4. Just what could be meant by N.'s phrase is startlingly illustrated by the so-called *Laudatio Turiae* (ed. E. Wistrand (Göteborg 1976), 25; cf. Horsfall, *BICS* 30 (1983), 91 f.).

12. 3. Lucius Saufeius. A knight, though there are several senatorial Saufeii (Nicolet, ii (1974), 1012 f.). The family may be from Praeneste (Palestrina). His wealth was clearly a temptation to the triumvirs, though his non-participation in politics and his Epicureanism are evident from the many references in Cicero's letters from 67 to 44 (cf. Shackleton Bailey on 1. 3. 1). Momigliano is reluctant to see his sojourn in Athens as politically innocent (*JRS* 31 (1941), 152), but Epicurean beliefs need not necessarily be politically significant (cf. note on 17. 3, **philosophers**). His name is found on a list of those honouring the philosopher Phaedrus (A. Raubitschek, *Hesp.* 18 (1949), 96 ff.), an Epicurean whom Cicero and Atticus knew in both Greece and Rome (he was probably at Rome from shortly before 88 until just after Sulla restored order at Athens in 86; cf. note on 2. 2 (**Athens**) for Atticus himself, and Raubitschek, op. cit. p. 98). There were statues to Saufeius at both Athens (*IG.* ii² 3897) and Tusculum (*CIL* xiv. 2624). One interesting fragment (on the development of civilization) is preserved (by Servius Dan. on *Aen.* 1. 6): cf. Rawson (1985), 9 n. 28.

philosophy. In the earliest stages, Greek philosophers came to Rome as ambassadors (cf. notes on Nepos, fr. 56 and Atticus, fr. 8), and Romans might study with Greeks in Rome (Panaetius, Blossius, Diophanes; cf. Rawson (1985), 6, 79 f.; Bonner (1977), 23 ff.). T. Albucius went to study in Athens and was excoriated by Lucilius (E. Warmington, *Remains of Old Latin*, iii. 18 ff.). Atticus was nearly, but not quite, the first distinguished Roman to settle in the Greek world to pursue philosophical interests (Rawson (1985), 6; Bonner (1977), 90 ff.); Crassus the orator (see note on 1. 4, **Torquatus**) no more than paused briefly (Rawson (1985), 6). Neither Atticus nor Cicero went as young as later visitors conventionally did (e.g. Horace at about twenty: Bonner (1977), 90). And clearly both Atticus and Saufeius stayed much longer than was usual. Cf. L. W. Daly, *AJPh* 71 (1950), 40 ff.

valuable estates. It was the Sullan proscriptions that particularly enriched private individuals; in 43–2 too much money was needed to pay off the troops. Wealth led many to be included: cf. note on 12. 4 (**in Africa**), and for Varro see note on 10. 2, (**shortly before**). See further RH, *ARE* i. 72 ff.; Syme (1939), 195; Horsfall, *BICS* 30, (1983), 92.

inheritance. Cf. notes on 12. 4 (**aide-de-camp** and **in Africa**) considering a comparable story.

12. 4. Lucius Julius Calidus. Perhaps the same man from whom
Cicero in 56 wrote a letter of recommendation (*Fam.* 13. 6a) to the
proconsul of Africa (cf. note on this section, **in Africa**) where N.'s
Calidus has property. And wealth does (cf. note on 12. 3, **valuable
estates**) encourage the proscribers. N.'s judgement on Calidus'
literary powers does appear to refer to a period just after the deaths
of Catullus and Lucretius (i.e. the late 50s); no poet of this name, or
a name nearly this, is otherwise known, let alone a figure
distinguished enough to merit the solemn encomium that N. offers
(cf. note on Nepos, fr. 58 for N. on Cicero). Worse, the syntax is
extremely entangled. Insufficient attention has been given to the
problem, or problems. Possibly N., despite the attactive coincidence
of the reference in Cicero, never referred to Calidus and a reference
to his name has by a chain of accidents come to replace that of the
brilliant neoteric poet C. Licinius Calvus (cf. C. Cichorius, *Römische
Studien* (Leipzig 1922), 88 f.), who was dead by 46. N. had once been
close to Catullus, and here manages an elegant passing compliment
to his dead friend (cf. note on *Praef.* 8, **haste**); his judgement on the
third poet of the age is not likely therefore to have been uninformed,
and an allusion here to a mysterious nonentity would be very
difficult.

Lucretius and Catullus. Cicero and his brother knew Lucretius'
poetry (*QF* 2. 9. 3) and Cicero may have edited Lucretius' poem for
publication, though the evidence (Jerome) is late and all details are
hotly disputed (cf. Lucretius, ed. C. Bailey, i. 18 ff.; A. Dalzell,
CHCL ii. 213, 833). That is, N. might have got to know Lucretius
through Cicero. Lucretius and Catullus are similarly paired at Vell.
2. 36. 2. For Catullus on N. cf. note on Nep. fr. 2.

and . . . knowledge. Cf. 1. 2 with note (**instructed**) for Atticus'
own father teaching him (*Epam.* 1. 4, *Dion* 1. 2). The phrase means
no more than 'very well educated'.

aide-de-camp. Volumnius was fortunately much in Atticus' debt:
cf. note on 9. 4 (**Volumnius**); the kindness had been in part
returned already (see note on 10. 2, **shortly before**). Cf. note on 10. 4
(**the proscribed**) for the proscription of the knights, and note on
9. 4 (**Volumnius**) for *praefectus fabrum* as 'aide-de-camp'.

in Africa. Our evidence for Romans holding estates in North Africa
at this date (collected by R. M. Haywood, *ESAR* iv. 29, including
Cicero's friend Caelius) is scanty, but that is probably no more than
a quirk in the transmission of the facts (Shatzman (1975), 34).

13. 1. But . . . citizen. The one major break in the first edition of the life; what precedes is not strictly chronological by any means (cf. pp. 9–10); what follows covers habits and written works, and corresponds closely to chapter 3 of the life of Cato. The content of chapter 14 corresponds closely to what we are told about book 1 of the autobiography of M. Aemilius Scaurus (cf. p. 10 n. 13, and Rawson (1985), 227 for details of what he had inherited). With the opening words of this chapter we might also compare the panegyric of L. Caecilius Metellus, *cos.* 251, 247, quoted by Plin. *NH* 7. 140. Cf. Steidle (1951), 149; Plut. *Cat. mai.* 21; Petr. 71.

building. We should remember that N. is writing at the same time as Sallust and Horace (*Serm.* 1, *Epodes* in particular); 'buying and building' is characteristic of the luxury the moralists excoriate. For the former cf. Sall. *Cat.* 11. 4 f.; Hor. *Carm.* 3. 24, *Ep.* 2. 2. 158 f.; Shatzman (1975), 24, 94 f.; d'Alton (1917; still very useful), 167 ff.: for the latter Sall. *Cat.* 12. 3; Hor. *Ep.* 1. 1. 100, *Carm.* 3. 1. 33 ff., 3. 24. 2 f.; d'Alton (1917), 174 ff.; Frank, *ESAR* i. 371 ff.; Shatzman, loc. cit.; Suet. *Caes.* 46. 1 gives a remarkable example from the recent past.

he . . . best. Cf. note on 13. 5 (**His . . . excess**) for some contemporary examples of the sort of great but discreet comfort about which N. is talking. 13. 3–6 and 14. 2 are rather prolix but the antitheses point repeatedly at the (originally Peripatetic) idea of 'the mean', the just balance between extremes of luxury and squalor; this becomes explicit at 13. 5 'his furnishings were moderate, not copious' ('supellex modica, non multa'). An idea particularly dear to Horace (*Serm.* 1. 1. 106, 2. 2. 112–15, *Carm.* 1. 20. 1, 2. 16. 9 ff., 3. 1. 25).

13. 2. Tamphilus'. The name of an early or distinguished owner clings to the house; cf. S. B. Platner and T. Ashby, *Topographical Dictionary of Ancient Rome* (Oxford 1929), 264 ff. *passim*. The name clearly refers to one of the many Baebii Tamphili.

grounds. No attempt to rival the urban architectural splendours of Crassus, Pompey, or Lucullus, but the existence of a 'silva' (see note on 14. 3, **park**) at this date on the Esquiline suggests that the grounds dated back to a time when the city had not spread beyond the Servian walls. One is not surprised to find Atticus enjoying a *rus in urbe*, quiet grounds surrounded by urban bustle. The site is clear enough: that now occupied by the Palazzo della Consulta, facing the main entrance to the Quirinal Palace. Cf. P. Grimal, *Les Jardins romains*[2] (Paris 1969), 104, 302 ff.

character. Literally, 'salt'!

luxury. It appears that the property still belonged to Pomponii under Trajan (*CIL* vi. 1492). 'Silva' can refer to what we might call a park or plantation: Cic. *Att.* 12. 31. 2; Verg. *G.* 4. 329; Prop. 3. 2. 13; and Sen. *Ep.* 64. 2 'beneath this shrub I was imagining the parks of the rich'!

13. 3. slave household. We are well informed on the structure and workings of large slave households at Rome and they have recently attracted much attention. For Cicero cf. Treggiari (1969), 252 ff. In general see Balsdon (1969), 106 ff.; Griffin (1985), 29 ff.; S. Treggiari, *PBSR* 43 (1975), 48 ff.; ead., *AJAH* 1. (1976), 76 ff. Some details will emerge shortly.

beauty. Beautiful slaves of varied ages and genders are almost too common in both poetry and life to require detailed comment: Q. Haterius the jurist remarked (Sen. *Contr.* 4. pr. 10, defending a freedman accused of being his patron's lover) 'immodest conduct is a crime in a free man, necessity in a slave, duty in a freedman.' Cf. Griffin (1985), 24 ff.; Hor. *Carm.* 1. 4. 19 with Nisbet and Hubbard's note; S. Treggiari, *PBSR* 43 (1975), 53 f.; ead. (1969), 211 f.; S. Lilja, *Homosexuality in Republican and Augustan Rome* (Helsinki 1983), 30 ff.

highly-educated slaves. They may be subdivided into various specialist activities: secretaries, library clerks, readers (cf. next note), copyists, papyrus technicians (as we might have to call them), and others: cf. Treggiari (1969), 147 ff.; ead., *PBSR* 43 (1975), 56; ead., *AJAH* 1 (1976), 78, 90 f. For the various jobs they undertook on the evidence of Cicero's letters see Byrne (1920), 27 f.; A. J. Marshall, *Phoen.* 30 (1976), 257 (an important study of how library resources conditioned research at the time); Treggiari (1969), 149.

readers. Both men and women, normally, for readings not only at dinner (cf. note on 14. 1), but in the bath; several are attested in inscriptions: Treggiari (1969), 148; ead., *AJAH* 1 (1976), 90; *PBSR* 30 (1975), 56, 74.

copyists. Cicero refers to Atticus' slaves checking references, copying, sticking rolls together; Atticus is still often described as a 'publisher' (e.g. Treggiari (1969), 149) and publishing is given as a source of his income (Finley (1973), 52). That is exceedingly unlikely: he made available his library, his specialist slaves, and particularly his copyists, to obtain, transcribe, or multiply works for his many friends. Numerous expert slaves could clearly produce many copies for a close friend (i.e. Cicero); that does not make Atticus what we may properly call a publisher, and there is no evidence at all that he made money thereby. His activity in the world of books is to be seen, as elsewhere, in terms of friendship and the return of favours. Cf. Rawson (1985), 43 f.; E. J. Kenney, *CHCL* ii. 20; J. J. Phillips, *CW* 79 (1986), 227 ff. is incautious.

so . . . finely. A mild pleasantry: footmen were expected to be large and strong. Cf. Catul. 10. 14 ff.; Treggiari (1969), 145 ff. It was unusual if one slave performed more than one job (cf. ead., *AJAH* 1 (1976), 93; ead., *PBSR* 30 (1975), 71 n. 137; Plin. *Ep.* 5. 19. 3; Mart. 3. 58; *Dig.* 32. 65. 2), indeed it could be represented as positively cheeseparing (Cic. *Pis.* 67), N. does not conceal (cf. note on 13. 6, **all ranks**) that Atticus was rather close in some of his ways.

good. In the imperial household (we are best informed on Livia's slaves), a huge number of slaves were maintained, with minute specialization of roles: Griffin (1985), 15; Treggiari, *PBSR* 30 (1975), 48 ff.; P. R. C. Weaver, *Familia Caesaris* (Cambridge 1972).

13. 4. in the household. Specialist slaves were extremely expensive if bought ready-trained; it was far more practical (and was thought safer, too) to train them at home (as Atticus clearly did) or to pay for their training. Cf. Bonner (1977), 37 f.; Balsdon (1969), 112; Frank, *ESAR* i. 380 ff.; and notably C. A. Forbes, *TAPA* 86 (1955), 337 ff.

this . . . desires. Language dear to N.: cf. *Cato* 3. 4. The 'not immoderate desires' are in the familiar terms of contemporary moralists: Hor. *Epod.* 3. 19; Sall. *Cat.* 11. 3, 51. 33.

determination. Cf. notes on 13. 3 (**so . . . finely** and **good**); in Atticus' household, slaves were, after all, trained in more than one specialist skill.

13. 5. He . . . elegance. Cf. 13. 1–4, 15. 1–2; the antitheses here are used sparingly and with some dexterity.

His . . . excess. Cf. note on 13. 1 (**he . . . best**). The word I translate as 'furnishings' is 'supellex', which readers of Horace (*Serm.* 1. 6. 118, *Ep.* 1. 5. 7) will think of as 'tableware', but that sense is not common; it usually means 'furnishings' and is defined in minute detail by Paulus at *Dig.* 33. 10. 3. Suetonius (*Aug.* 73. 1) comments on the 'parsimony of his furniture and fittings' which appears 'even now in the couches and tables that survive; most of them are hardly worthy of the elegance of a private individual'; he likewise wore home-made clothing. With N.'s account here it is also interesting to compare Cicero on Antony (*Phil.* 2. 66) and Plutarch on Pompey (40. 5).

13. 6. trivial. Cf. note on *Praef.* 1 (**that . . . men**); N. is disquieted lest people should think ill of the discrepancy between Atticus' greatness as a man and the frivolity of the domestic detail he provides. We in turn think of such detail as conveying valuable information on social and economic history, and such illuminating social minutiae are something in which N. is clearly interested (cf. p. xviii n. 18). It no longer matters at all that the dignity of great public affairs is lacking.

substantial. Literally, 'well-washed' ('lautus'), hence 'respectable', 'substantial', even 'luxurious'; with N.'s use here, cf. Cic. *Att.* 8. 1. 3.

all ranks. 'You give us bits of cabbage for dinner on fern-pattern dishes and in magnificent baskets. What can I expect you to serve on earthenware?' (Cic. *Att.* 6. 1. 13, cf. 16. 3. 1; SB i. 57 n. 12): it is no surprise to learn that Atticus was not a lavish host. For his dinners cf. further notes on 14. 1. For dinner invitations cf. Balsdon (1969), 32 ff. Atticus was not alone in enjoying a wide social range; so, notably Marcus Crassus the triumvir (Plut. *Crass.* 2. 7) and similarly, the farcical dinner described in Hor. *Serm.* 2. 8. Augustus appears to have been more exclusive: see Suet. *Aug.* 74. 1.

3,000 sesterces. The MSS here give 3,000 asses, not HS, per month, a quarter as much at this date; that can hardly be right, for it would have paid only for 48 litres of fine wine (at the prices of 89; see Plin. 14. 95). Even 3,000 HS seems a very modest sum, until it is realized that much produce must have been brought in from the estate at Mentana (cf. note on 14. 3, **no . . . sea**). Cf. Frank, *ESAR* i. 402 ff. for some contemporary prices.

his accounts. The evidence for monthly accounts, which Cicero claims with scorn that C. Fannius Chaerea should have kept (*Rosc. Com.* 3–8; cf. *II Verr.* 1. 60–1; it was clearly not done not to keep them) is discussed by G. E. M. de Sainte Croix in *Studies in the History of Accounting* (London 1956), 42 ff.; cf. A. Watson, *The Law of*

Obligations (Oxford 1965), 38. N. does not make clear whether he has seen the ledgers, or has been told what they show; he does, though, make it clear that there is written evidence behind his claim (p. 7) to autopsy.

13. 7. This . . . relations. Geiger *Lat.* 44 (1985), 262 is probably right to suggest that N. met Atticus through Cicero; for their relations, cf. p. xv; 'relations' translates 'familiaritas', which is not a word used of close friendship, as emerges clearly from 19. 2, 4; cf. *Ages.* 1. 1, *Eum.* 4. 4. Contrast 'convictus' (see note on 8. 2, **daily companion**). Was N. present at Atticus' death? Cf. note on 21. 5 (**health**).

14. 1. reader. For specialist readers cf. note on 13. 3 (**readers**); Atticus clearly did not have musicians at dinner; many did. But reading was a common form of entertainment at table: Balsdon (1969), 44 f.; Rawson (1985), 51. Augustus' tastes were less austere (Suet. *Aug.* 84).

nor . . . bellies. The one modest jest; perhaps one of Atticus' own. At 1. 3 humour has been sought, wrongly; cf. note on that section (**equanimity**). The robustly entertaining Cato is efficiently sterilized; cf. p. 4. Livy (cf. 7. 10. 5) has perceptibly the same aversion. Comparison with Plutarch, Suetonius, or John Aubrey is instructive. Atticus was by no account a dull man, and the life suffers from the lack of verbal detail, though some sayings may be unobtrusively preserved (cf. p. 13).

14. 2. for . . . own. Cf. 10. 2 (Kanus), 12. 3 (Saufeius), 12. 4 ('Calidus'), 19. 2 (Octavian) for the motif of friends of similar taste, familiar also in theoretical writing about friendship (cf. notes on 5. 3, **ties of blood** and 19. 2, **he . . . state**).

same level. For a very similar picture of equanimity in the face of wealth cf. Hor. *Serm.* 2. 2. 113–14. N. mentions only 2 legacies (of many, see note on 21. 1, **legacies**; sixteen received by Cicero are known; see Shatzman (1975), 409 ff.); he gives no idea of just how successful Atticus' dealings and investments were, and indeed gives no clear picture of the real basis of his wealth (cf. note on 14. 3, **income**, for this problem). N. calls Atticus 'pecuniosus', 'moneyed' and 'splendidus' (13. 1, 5). We have some idea of what might count as great wealth in the late republic (Frank, *ESAR* i. 393 f.): a 'sumptuosus' ('lavish') might have an income of 600,000 HS a year (Cic. *Parad.* 49); cf. Garnsey (1976), 126; Finley (1973), 55.

14. 3. park. The 'silva' (13. 2) of his house on the Quirinal (cf. note on 13. 2, **grounds**) was clearly something far more modest; '*horti* are more than mere "gardens"' (N. Purcell, in *Ancient Roman Villa Gardens* (Dumbarton Oaks 1987), 203). Rather, an extensive suburban property on the very edge of the city. For details, cf. Grimal, *Les Jardins romains*, 2 107 ff.

no . . . sea. Cf. E. Rawson in M. I. Finley (ed.), *Studies in Roman Property* (Cambridge 1976), 92 f.; Shatzman (1975), 24 f.; Purcell in *Ancient Roman Villa Gardens*. The suburban villa is not only pleasant and convenient; it feeds the owner while he is in Rome (cf. note on 13. 6, **3,000 sesterces**) and may yield some profit. For the seaside villa see in particular J. D'Arms, *Romans on the Bay of Naples* (Cambridge, Mass. 1970) and M. Frederiksen, *Campania* (BSR 1984), 335 *et passim*: again, pleasure and profitability are conjoined. It is not quite clear (cf. next note) that N.'s statement here is true.

Mentana. He thought (Cic. *Att.* 4. 8. 1, 9. 9. 4) of buying others. Ibid. 12. 34. 1 refers to a villa at Ficulea; ibid. 7. 3. 6, 12. 36. 2, 37. 2, 38. 1, 40. 5 refer to a 'suburban' villa; there are no other references to a villa at Nomentum (Mentana, 16 miles north of Rome, just east of the Tiber valley). It is possible that all these texts refer to one and the same property; the ancient Via Nomentana passed through Ficulea. In that case, N. protests too much: Atticus did have a villa that Cicero repeatedly called 'suburban'; to say that it was not was to exalt Atticus' frugality at the expense of common sense!

income. The estate near Buthrotum was acquired in 68; there was other property on the coast of Epirus, on Corcyra, and on the Sybota Islands (Drumann, 65 f.). But there is no other reliable evidence in the *Letters to Atticus* that he owned urban property (Byrne (1920), 12 f.; Garnsey (1976), 125 f.; see however P. A. Brunt, *Second International Conference on Economic History, Aix 1962*, i. (1965), 128 = Seager (1969), 94), or derived income from it. His occasional interest in it may be explained if it could serve as surety for loans he made. But it is what N. leaves out that is so remarkable: there are very extensive loans and business interests throughout the Aegean; the loan to Sicyon (Cic. *Att.* 1. 13. 1 etc.) was a major preoccupation (Shackleton Bailey ad loc.; cf. in general Byrne (1920), 3 ff.), in contrast to the 'friendly' loans to Athens (cf. note on 2. 4, **when . . . terms**). In Rome 'publishing' is best left out of the discussion (cf. note on 13. 3, **copyists**). Not so dealing in gladiators and in other skilled slaves (Cic. *Att.* 4. 17. 6; Byrne (1920), 13 f.; Lintott (1968), 83 ff.; Wiseman (1971), 79). He also lent money (e.g. to Metellus

(Cic. *Att.* 4. 7. 2) and Q. Cicero (Drumann, 68)), and was active in other banking operations (though the activities mentioned in 15. 2 (cf. note on that section, **if . . . perform**) cannot have been directly profitable). It is clear that Atticus had an exceptional head for business (Cic. *Att.* 7. 1. 2); and N. does not disguise (see note on 2. 4) that he was not hindered by considerations of generosity or sentiment (cf. Drumann, 85 f.) in his formal transactions. The sequence of thought in 14. 2–3 might suggest that N. wishes implicitly to convey the overall impression that Atticus received two legacies, totalling 12 m. HS, which he invested wisely in property. Of all the other financial interests, not a word, explicitly: 15. 3 does not refer to a source of regular income. N., that is, may invent the urban property and suppress most of what we can extract from Cicero about the real sources and scale of Atticus' wealth. Why? Money at Rome attracted reactions of snobbery and circumlocution: cf. D'Arms (1981), 60; Wiseman (1971), 82 n. 2; cf. Garnsey (1976), 124 (but can N. have been that ill informed?); Shatzman (1975), 379. The question is in part one of 'image'; Atticus had clearly learned from his savage old uncle (cf. note on 5. 1, **Quintus Caecilius**). He became himself a consummate business man, but the long story of the 'siege of Sicyon', for example, presents utterly the wrong picture: N.'s outlook is far closer to the confusing idealism of Cic. *Off.* 1. 151 (cf. note on this section, **reason**): Atticus is to be presented as living from the income of his landed property; other sources of wealth may, if 'respectable', be mentioned in passing (21. 1, **legacies**). It is easy enough, therefore, to see why N. throws dust in our eyes; he could hardly have brought himself to do otherwise. Contrast D'Arms (1981), 100 ff, a brilliant analysis of how Petronius presents the sources of Trimalchio's wealth.

Epirus and Rome. Cf. the beginning of the previous note.

reason. Note Finley (1973), 41 ff. for an analysis of Cicero's famous evaluation in moral terms of possible sources of income (*Off.* 1. 150 ff.).

15. 1. Lies . . . endure. Note a contemporary definition: 'the difference between "to tell a lie" ['mendacium dicere'] and "to lie" ['mentiri'] is: he who lies is himself not deceived, but tries to deceive another; he who tells a lie is himself deceived . . . the good man should ensure that he does not lie, the wise that he does not tell a lie' (Nigidius Figulus, quoted by Gell. 11. 11). Shackleton Bailey (i. 58) notes smilingly that Atticus was capable of prudent dissimulation. But there is a serious point behind N.'s emphatic statement. In the light of contemporary discussion of the art of lying (Cic. *Off.* 3. 61, 82; id., *De orat.* 3. 113), it is clear that Atticus will have thought that it was essential to his business activities and reputation that his name for *fides*, 'trust', should be entirely unblemished; note that N. returns shortly to Atticus' sense of his word as his bond.

charm. 'Your life and talk', says Cicero himself (*Leg.* 3. 1), 'seem to have attained that most difficult combination of gravity and humanity'; Cicero writes a letter of recommendation for one Sex. Aufidius (*Fam.* 12. 27): he combines the utmost severity with the utmost humanity.

respected or loved. Cf. Cic. *Am.* 82 for open acknowledgement of the importance of an element of respect (again 'vereor') in friendship; 'verecundia', the abstract quality of the man who feels what I have translated as 'respect' is equivalent to the Greek *aidos*. 'Amare' I translate simply as 'love'; it can (Hellegouarc'h (1963), 142 f.) refer to no more than political alliance, but also covers the whole range of affection and love (Brunt (1965), 1 ff. = Seager (1969), 199 ff.).

If . . . perform. The sequence of thought in this paragraph is organized tightly; N. presents Atticus as having a sense of scruple ('religio') about undertaking to perform a service ('officium') that leads to exceptional care ('cura', 15. 2) in executing the 'mandata' of his friends. N. is writing in the terms of such discussions as we find in Cic. *Off.* 3. 104, and notably *Rosc. Am.* 111. Cicero refers often to Atticus' 'diligentia' (Att. 1. 9. 2, 2. 4. 1, 7. 3. 1, etc.). A *mandatum* (which I translate 'commission', 15. 2) should be in law gratuitous (A. Watson, *Law of Obligations* (Oxford 1965), 150; but not, to Atticus, unrewarding in the long run (cf. note on 21. 1, **legacies**). See Crook (1969), 237 for a lucid survey of the law of mandate, 'the contract by which one man undertook the affairs of another on instructions'; we should, though, remember that literary texts (such as N. here) do not use words such as 'mandate' or 'looked after' in their precise and technical legal sense.

15. 2. dearer. Cicero and Atticus were not always satisfied with each other's devotion in matters of business (SB i. 19 f.); but cf. compliments such as Cic. *Att.* 12. 37. 3, 13. 13. 1. What was involved? 'Collecting debts, supervising the quality of coin in payments, witnessing and executing wills, attending or conducting sales, making purchases or investments, placing loans with other bankers, issuing bills of exchange' (Byrne (1920), 11; cf. further SB i.

8; Crook (1969), 237, Brunt (1965), 6 = Seager (1969), 204; Shatzman (1975), 188). Oppius, Matius, and (cf. note on 21. 4, **Lucius . . . him**) Balbus did the same sort of thing for Caesar, Cluvius for Pompey, and possibly Caecilius for Lucullus (cf. note on 4. 5, **escorted**): it saved time, trouble, and dignity for great public men to conduct their business thus. Atticus thought his reputation (*existimatio*) at stake: that is, his business conduct greatly affected the public esteem in which he was held by his peers; cf. Z. Yavetz, *Julius Caesar and his Public Image* (London 1983), 216. The law recognizes that the conduct of *mandatum* involves a man's *existimatio* (*Cod. Iust.* 4. 35. 21).

15. 3. So . . . besides. For relations with the Ciceros cf. notes on 5. 2–3; Atticus was exceptionally fond of Cato (cf. Cic. *Att.* 1. 17. 9; 2. 1. 8; SB i. 7 n. 3; cf. also Geiger (1985), 106 and note on *Cato* 3. 5 **Atticus** for the bearing of Atticus' relations with Cato upon N.'s *Cato*); cf. 5. 4 with notes for Hortensius, and 11. 2 for A. Torquatus.

choice. Atticus had a most active interest in politics (see note on 8. 4, **dissent**), and could exert great weight: he could, that is, participate without commitment. There were others so positioned (cf. note on 13. 3, **beauty**).

16. 1. humanity. Cf. note on 4. 1 (**culture and learning**) for *humanitas*, a motif of this life, not its central theme.

Sulla . . . Brutus. For Atticus' relations with Sulla cf. 4. 1–2 with notes; with Brutus cf. 8. 1–2 with notes; for Hortensius 5. 4 with notes. N. here summarizes earlier notices; Atticus' ability to cross generation boundaries in his friendships has already been observed.

16. 2. closer. For the Ciceros cf. 5. 3: clearly, N. has allowed an uneconomical and repetitious degree of overlap between the two 'halves' of the life (cf. p. 9), which he did not see fit to remove in the (cf. p. 8 f.) second edition.

16. 3. books. Atticus was the dedicatee of the *De amicitia* and *De senectute* (cf. p. 79); in the *De legibus*, *Brutus*, *Academica posteriora*, and *De finibus* he has a speaking role.

published. The evidence has often been collected: cf. most recently Phillips, *CW*, 79 (1986) 231 ff.; Rawson (1985), 43 ff., and note on 13. 3 (**copyists**) for a warning about the limited sense in which 'published' is to be understood. Atticus is essential to Cicero from the first reading he undertakes for one of his philosophical or rhetorical works, through verification of detail of all kinds, to final copying and distribution on a limited scale. Cf., (e.g.) Cic. *Att.* 4. 14. 1; 16. 2; 5. 12. 2; 6. 1. 8; 6. 2. 3 f., 9; 6. 3. 3; those are but the main references to the genesis of Cicero's *De republica*.

letters. The letters of which N. writes are clearly as yet unpublished; the MSS of N. give 11 books, not the 16 that we now have; they date from Cicero's consulship (63), says N., to his death. But we have 11 earlier letters and none (cf. note on 9. 3, **Cicero**) from the last months of his life. The 11 rolls that N. saw may have been (SB i. 72) a selection Atticus made for his friends. What we now have is, clearly enough, something else. See the exemplary and magisterial discussion at SB i. 60 ff.; R. S. Stewart, *TAPA* 93 (1962), 469 ff. still thinks N. saw the collection we have. On the date of publication of the collection see the entertaining paper by A. Setaioli, *Symb. Osl.* 51 (1976), 105 ff.

period. The collection *Ad Att.* as we have it is largely in chronological sequence (SB i. 69); 'continuous' 'contextam', literally 'woven together' a rare expression, used (e.g.) by Orosius of Tacitus (*Hist.* fr. 6 Fisher); it is unlikely that N. means anything more than 'continuous'.

16. 4. for . . . state. 'A foolish exaggeration (Shackleton Bailey, *Cicero* (London 1971), p. xii). Justly said: N. is easily carried away, and lacks a sober controlling judgement.

that . . . use. Cf. the problem of 'divinatio' at 9. 1 (**character of a seer**). Here it may be that 'prudentia', which I translate as 'good sense' is used, as it is elsewhere, though rarely, to mean 'foresight' (cf. Cic. *Sen.* 78, Verg. *Aen.* 3. 433; i.e. much the same as 'providentia'). Nor is it quite clear whether 'divinatio', which I render as an adjective, 'prophetic', should refer rather to some less dramatic quality such as 'foresight' or 'anticipation'—so, perhaps, 'prescient' in the text. But fiddle as we may, N.'s exaggeration and folly remain.

17. 1. devotion. *Pietas*: devotion to gods, state, and family, exemplified by the conduct of Virgil's Aeneas: discussion, stifled by excess, has ground to a halt. Cf. the summary and bibliography by R. G. Austin at *Aen.* 1. 10. The lapidary good sense of W. Warde Fowler (*Death of Turnus* (Oxford 1919), 146 ff.; id., *Religious Experience* *of the Roman People* (London 1922), 409 ff. has not been bettered. On the history of the idea cf. Bremmer and Horsfall (1987), 13 ff.

mother's funeral. On Atticus' mother cf. note on 2. 1 (**father**). The funeral speech was delivered by a near relative, or, quite often, by a distinguished orator known to the family. Cf. Horsfall, *BICS* 30 (1983), 89 ff.; Kennedy (1972), 21 ff.; Wistrand, '*Laudatio Turiae*'.

sixty-seven. Atticus was 67 when his mother died in 42, a widow for half a century; she had outlived her nasty brother by sixteen years (see note on 5. 2, **three-quarters**). For a comparable lifespan cf. N.'s oral source, M. Perperna (see note on *Cato*, 1. 1, **Perperna**), and Plin. *NH* 7. 156–9: unusual, not incredible.

contemporary. For his irritable sister and her ill-starred marriage, cf. note on 5. 3 (**match**).

17. 2. wicked. This tamely renders 'nefas', since such anger would have been a breach of *pietas*, of Atticus' sense of the depth of devotion he owed to his close kin. 'Nefas' N. used of the Roman view of marriage with a half-sister (see note on Foreign Generals 4, **outrage**); Virgil applies it to the very idea that Aeneas could have left Troy without Anchises (*Aen.* 2. 658). The episode narrated at Cic. *Att.* 5. 1. 4 (cf. Hallett (1984), 172; SB i. 57) suggests that Pomponia must have been a notably heavy cross for Atticus to bear; no hint in the letters that he was not up to it.

17. 3. alone. A passing reflection of an old debate: do we become good from something within ourselves or is it something that we learn? Discussion found as early as Thgn. 429 ff.; Pl. *Men.* 70a. For the history of the debate (notably in the hands of the Sophists) see Guthrie (1969), 55 ff.; still a matter for discussion when N. was writing (cf. Cic. *Part. Or.* 64; id. *Am.* 6; id., *Arch.* 15; id., *Fin.* 3. 11, 4. 21, 5. 59; Hor. *Ep.* 1. 18. 100).

philosophers. Atticus' interest in Epicureanism may have begun under Phaedrus at Rome (though cf. E. Badian, *AJAH* 1 (1976), 114) before ever he went to Athens (cf. note on 12. 3, **Lucius Saufeius**); at Athens he followed both Epicurean and other lectures; those of Antiochus the Academic remained a serious and lasting influence (Cic. *Fin.* 5. 1, *Leg.* 1. 54). N.'s disdain for philosophy is well attested (cf. pp. 119) and here he does not mention Epicurus by name, though elsewhere he repeats accurately some specifically Epicurean language (cf. p. xvi). Nor indeed was Atticus passionately

committed; he wrote no philosophy, unlike his friend Saufeius; he
kept no resident sage, unlike Cicero; he is not known to have
accepted the dedication of Epicurean treatises; he had no special
interest in Epicurean books. There is no obvious community of
thought or interest between Atticus and either the early popularizing
Epicureans (cf. notes on Nepos, fr. 58 and on 12. 4, **Lucretius**)
Of his friends mentioned in the life, Saufeius was Epicurean; so too
Cassius (*Fam.* 15. 19; for others, cf. Nicolet, i (1966), 710). Cicero
jokes easily to Atticus at the Epicureans' expense (*Att.* 14. 20. 5, 15.
4. 2), but can represent him in the *De finibus* and *De legibus* as a
credible and eloquent holder of Epicurean views. Epicurean beliefs
did not (cf. note on 10. 8, **but . . . remarkable**) entail a particular
political allegiance, nor indeed is Epicurean doctrine on political
involvement quite decisive and unambiguous (cf. Lucr. 1. 40 f.; Sen.
De otio 3. 2; Cic. *De orat.* 3. 63; M. Griffin, *Seneca* (Oxford 1976), 344).
Saufeius appears to have taken non-participation further than
Atticus. Atticus' devotion to friendship and a sober life-style
(chapters 13–14) were characteristic of serious Epicureans (the term
is misused in current parlance), but would not have caused surprise
in a Stoic. The same (cf. note on 21. 5, **own interests**) applied to his
death. It is easy to understand men (whether the uncommitted
Atticus or the moderate Caesarian Matius) who preferred the
realities of power, wealth, and influence to the hazards and illusions
of office. N.'s silence about Atticus' philosophical allegiance is at the
outset surprising, but becomes far more understandable when we
realize that that allegiance was not decisive; more important, N.
saw rightly (cf. next note) that Atticus took practical ethics very
seriously. Cf. Byrne (1920), 23 ff.; Nicolet, i (1966), 707 ff.; Rawson
(1985), 284 f.; and the fine pages of P. Grimal, *Actes Assoc. G. Budé,* 8
(1969), 139 ff.

life. It should be recognized that philosophical reflection was an
active and integral part of life: that is clear both from the explicitly
meditative Horace and, more strikingly, from its obvious and
natural place on occasion in the corpus of Cicero's letters (consolation
and condolence are the obvious contexts): cf. *Fam.* 3. 7. 5, 4. 5, 5. 13.
1; Macleod, (1983), 281 f. = *JRS* 69 (1979), 17 f.

for show. N., we remember, is no friend to philosophy in general;
but Cicero too could make fun of extremes of Stoicism (Cato: *Mur.*
60–5) or Epicureanism (Piso: *Pis. passim;* cf. the index of R. G. M.
Nisbet's edition s.v.); on 'philosophy for show' cf. Cic. *Ac.* 2. 72; Sen.
Ep. 16. 3.

18. 1. ancestral custom. It is hard to find definition or discussion of *mos maiorum*. There are some helpful remarks in D. Earl, *Moral and Political Tradition of Rome* (London 1967), 28 *et passim*: Syme (1939), 315 f. Atticus, we should remember, was an optimate (6. 1, **optimates** and see notes on 6. 2, **traditional manner**), and did not change his ways (7. 3, end), nor his house (13. 2). The young Octavian realized (20. 2) that here was a real survivor, a man who knew intimately and himself embodied 'the old ways'. Atticus, through Octavian, is a link between the Scipionic circle and the principate (cf. note on 4. 1, **captured**)! As a boy he could have met a daughter of the elder Scipio Africanus (see note on *Letter of Cornelia*, **A . . . letter**), he lived to see his granddaughter engaged to the future emperor Tiberius.

antiquity. Cf. Cicero (*Brut.* 60) on Varro: 'our friend Varro, a most diligent investigator of antiquity'. But they are not to be paired: Atticus it will emerge (cf. Rawson (1985), 103, 231 f.), appears a rigorous and scrupulous scholar, a student of archival material, and devoted to exactitude in his representation of the past. Varro (cf. A. D. Momigliano, *Contributo* . . . (Rome 1955), 67 ff.; Rawson (1985), 233 ff.) accumulates huge quantities of information, new and old, correctly and confusedly; Varro, not Atticus, might have felt at home among Wood, Aubrey, and the English late seventeenth-century antiquaries.

volume . . . order. On the *Liber annalis* of Atticus (the title is often given wrongly; this is clearly its correct form), cf. the tributes of Cicero (*Brut.* 13 f. 'the book in which he covered the whole of history briefly, and so far as I can tell, very carefully . . the chronology was set out so that I could see it all at a glance' (tr. Douglas); *Orat.* 120 'this task [the orator's mastery of history] my friend Atticus' toil has relieved; he kept and indicated the dates, left out nothing important, and yet enclosed the record of seven hundred years in a single volume'). Broughton's *MRR*, its ultimate descendant, took three volumes. The fragments tell us disappointingly little (cf. p. 124); its real quality and influence appears from a study of Cicero's writing on historical matters before and after, and notably from the high accuracy of the history of oratory in the *Brutus*. Cf. E. Fantham *LCM* 6. 1 (1981), 17; Sumner (1973), 161 ff.; Rawson (1985), 103; ead., *JRS* 62 (1972) 40; Byrne (1920), 40 ff.; Douglas (1966), pp. lii ff.

18. 2. for . . . history. On the contents, N.'s information is confirmed elsewhere: when he mentions magistracies, we should remember that it appears that Atticus listed consuls and censors only, not praetors. For laws cf. Cic. *Sen.* 10, 14, *Am.* 96; for treaties id., *Sen.* 10; for important events id., *Brut.* 60; 'offspring' is what N. says ('propagines'): we expect 'ancestors', in view of Cicero's expertise in matters of filiation in his late works (e.g. *Brut.* 77–9) and of the familiar conventions for recording a man's father and grandfather (e.g. A. Postumius L.f. L.n. Albinus). But N. may mean that Atticus simply by giving information regularly in this form enabled the attentive reader to establish some at least of the descendants of famous men; there existed no abbreviated and conventionalized system for recording a man's progeny.

date. Roman chronology is now anchored to a foundation date of 753 (Cic. *Brut.* 72; Sol. 1. 27; cf. note on Nepos, fr. 9; so Varro, Atticus, and, after Atticus, Cicero); previously Cicero (*Rep.* 2. 18) preferred, after Polybius, Eratosthenes, and Apollodorus (see D.H. 1. 74. 3, Sol. 1. 27), and in agreement with Nep. *Chron.* (cf. Nepos, fr. 9), the second year of the seventh Olympiad, i.e. 751/0. Thereafter it appears clear that Atticus made reference by consular date exceptionally simple; Cicero (*Brut.* 15) stresses how easy the work was to use; it is tempting to suppose that, as in the Capitoline Fasti, there was a cross-reference to dating *ab urbe condita*, AVC, from the foundation of the city, every ten years; we should note, though, that the Fasti show interesting signs of not being influenced by the *Liber annalis* (F. Münzer, *Herm.* 40 (1905), 57; L. Ross Taylor, *CPh* 41 (1946), 10; Byrne (1920), 46).

offspring . . . men. Clearly there is a problem in 'offspring of famous men' (cf. note on 18. 2, **For . . . history**). There may be a Hellenistic antecedent: cf. Momigliano (1971), 85 and Rawson (1985), 232 for biographies of third-century BC Ptolemies in a genealogical context. Cf. further Sumner (1973), 165.

18. 3. families. There were ample family records in many cases; much of the material they contained is notoriously unreliable. But consultation did not make Atticus a perpetuator, like Varro, of charming genealogical fantasies (cf. Rawson (1985), 231 f.; Horsfall, *BICS* 30 (1983), 89 f.; T. P. Wiseman, *G&R* 21 (1974), 153 ff.).

present. Brutus and Atticus were friends by 51 (Cic. *Att.* 6. 1. 3; cf. note on 8. 2, **Marcus**), and the book's existence may already be implied by Cic. *Brut.* 109; Brutus appears to have had in his house a painted family tree, based on Atticus' researches (Cic. *Att.* 13. 40. 1 with Shackleton Bailey; cf. Rawson (1985), 96; Sumner (1973), 165). The descent claimed for M. Iunius Brutus from the original M.

Brutus the Liberator had been current in the family at least since 138 BC when a Decimus Brutus was consul and the tragedian Accius wrote a *Brutus*.

18. 4. Claudius Marcellus. M. Claudius Marcellus, *cos.* 51, died in 45; C. Claudius Marcellus, *cos.* 50 died in 40; and C. Claudius Marcellus, *cos.* 49, died before 43. N. gives no praenomen, which suggests that Atticus wrote at a time when there was only one consular Claudius Marcellus alive, so that the abbreviated form of the name would cause no confusion; after, that is, the death of the consul of 49 and before 40 when C. Claudius Marcellus, *cos.* 50, died; he was the first husband of Octavian's sister Octavia, and the father of the Marcellus lamented by Virgil (*Aen.* 6. 855 ff.); it is likely that Augustus' funeral speech on Marcellus, which was used by Virgil, was in turn indebted for its detail on family history to Atticus' book (cf. Plut. *Marc.* 30; Hor. *Carm.* 1. 12. 45; Prop. 3. 18. 33; Horsfall, *CR* 32 (1982), 37).

Fabii and Aemilii. N.'s phrasing does not place the matter beyond doubt, but it looks as though Atticus responded to a double request with a single work: the Fabius seems to be the consul of 45, who died on 31 December of that year (Cic. *Fam.* 7. 30. 1); the Scipio may be the suffect consul of 35 and not the Metellus Scipio who died after Thapsus (46); cf. Byrne (1920) 37 f. But see E. Badian in *Vir bonus discendi peritus*, *BICS* Suppl. 51 (1988), 9 with n. 16: from the discussion in Ann Marshall's Harvard 1986 thesis on Atticus, part of which she most kindly made available to me, the Scipio who approached Atticus seems likeliest to have been Cornelius Scipio Pomponianus Salvitto. Cf. further Plin. *NH* 35. 8; R. A. Billows, *AJAH* 7 (1982), 53 ff.

famous men. Not delightful biographical trivia, but rigorous prosopography; N. uses language more commonly applied to the 'soft' end of historiography, hugely popular in his day (E. Gabba in M. Crawford (ed.), *Sources for Ancient History* (Cambridge 1983), 13 ff., id., *JRS* 71 (1981), 50 ff.; Rawson (1985), 46, 215 ff.; Wiseman (1979), 3 ff.

18. 5. charm. It was positively unusual for Romans of good family at this date not to write some poetry, if they were of a literary bent: N. did (Plin. *Ep.* 5. 3. 6); so too Varro, Cicero, Augustus, Brutus, Hortensius, Sulla, Caesar (cf. Plin. *Ep.* loc. cit.; Gell. 19. 9. 7; Mart. 1 *Praef.*)

18. 6. portraits. 'The existence of a strong passion for portraits in former days is evidenced by Atticus the friend of Cicero in the volume he published on the subject and by the most benevolent invention of Marcus Varro who actually by some means inserted in a prolific output of volumes portraits of seven hundred famous people' (Plin. *NH* 35. 11, tr. H. Rackham, Loeb edn.). It is clear from Pliny that Varro was the first to put pictures and epigrams together in his text, and Varro's work is securely dated to 39 (cf. Momigliano (1981), 98; Geiger (1985), 82); N. suggests clearly enough that there were both verses and pictures in Atticus' text. The epigrams were clearly likely to be similar to Varro's, of which two survive (E. Baehrens, *Fragmenta poetarum Latinorum*, 295 f.). The subject-matter almost dictates that the epigrams must have been in Latin; those in the 'Amaltheum' of Atticus' estate in Epirus belong to 61–60 and were presumably in Greek (cf. Cic. *Att.* 1. 16. 15; F. G. Moore, *CPh* 1 (1906), 121). Varro was probably occupied on his collection of portraits already in 44; they were finished in 39 (Plin. *NH* 35. 11; Cic. *Att.* 16. 11. 3). Of N. himself, we know only that he was occupied on books 13–14 of the *De viris illustribus* in 35–32 (cf. Geiger (1985), 81; Rawson (1985), 231). The priority of Varro is therefore no more than likely. What the two works have in common is comparison of famous Greeks and Romans by category on a huge scale.

Cicero. 'A trifle rough and unkempt' said Cicero (*Att.* 2. 1. 1: i.e. without rhetorical elaboration); a paragraph later he relates that he has shown the great scholar Posidonius his own account, also in Greek (ibid. 1. 20. 6), of his consulship 'with the idea that he might compose something more elaborate on the same theme; so far from being stimulated to composition he was effectively frightened away.' And Cicero never realized the point of that reply!

19. 1. lifetime. Atticus died (see note on 22. 3, **fifth . . . consuls**) 31 March 32. For other traces of the second edition cf. p. 9 (repetition between the first edition and this appendix), p. 9 (the past tenses of chapters 13–18), and also *Reg.* 3. 5 and *Han.* 13. 1 for traces of a second edition elsewhere in the *De viris illustribus*. Cf. Geiger (1985), 85.

fortune. So Virgil has Aeneas say that Fortune has begrudged him Pallas, his comrade-in-arms and son of his ally Evander, prematurely killed by Turnus (*Aen.* 11. 43); cf. too Liv. 2. 12. 7.

LIFE OF ATTICUS p. 26

actual examples. Cf. 'recounting the Greeks' virtues' (*Praef.* 3.), and above all *Ages.* 4. 2 (on his obedience to orders from Sparta), 'an example that I only wish our generals had been willing to follow'. Cf. further note on *Cato*, 2. 2 (**law**).

as . . . fortune. Cf. note on 11. 6 (**each . . . fortune**); N. does not iron out the repetition.

19. 2. entered. Atticus' uncle Caecilius did not even necessarily begin life as an *eques*; he lives to see his granddaughter engaged to the future emperor Tiberius. The whole story, as N. quietly enough recognizes, is a fine warning against any ideas of rigid stratification and class structure at Rome. Cf. Hopkins, (1983), 110.

emperor. Octavian is *imperator* from 40 or 38; Syme (1939), 112 f.; Weinstock (1971), 103 ff. The case for 40 is argued in detail (on the basis of the Fasti Triumphales Barberiniani) by R. Combès, *Imperator* (Paris 1966), 134 f. By some time between 32 and 27 N. appears to be using the word in a sense that has shifted towards 'emperor'; the developments studied in R. Syme, *Roman Papers*, i (Oxford 1979), 361 ff. do not quite apply here.

deified. Julius was consecrated on or near 1 January 42 (Syme (1939), 202; Weinstock (1971), 386), but the title was used officially from the Peace of Brundisium (see note on 12. 1, **he . . . particular**), 40 BC; cf. Weinstock (1971), 399.

he . . . state. Note the awkward overlap with 12. 1–2. It is not quite clear whether Atticus knew Octavian (in 19. 3 and 19. 4 called 'Caesar') or Agrippa first (cf. also 20. 1); Atticus' relations with the young Octavian are described more fully than any of the friendships in the first edition (including that with Cicero!); N. has not been slow to realize that it will shortly prove extremely significant. Octavian was already of some education (cf. Suet. *Aug.* 84. 1; note on 12. 1, **Marcus Vipsanius**); he was to develop a powerful sense of the political relevance of history and of the use of the past to supply precedents which would enable him to present innovations as reversions (cf. Suet. *Aug.* 89. 2, 31. 4; Aug. *RG* 6. 1, 8. 5)! Atticus had captivated Octavian by his 'elegantia' (cf. 13. 5), which was a quality of mind as well as of taste. N. is notably careful in setting out in brief the basis of Atticus' more important friendships (cf. 4. 1, 5. 3, 10. 2, 12. 1).

19. 3. hitherto. N.'s tone about Octavian is not particularly admiring (cf. 12. 1, 20. 5): a distant appraisal of the realities of the young man's power. N. died after 27 (Plin. *NH* 9. 137); just when we cannot say. 'Prosperitas', which I translate as 'success' was not an idea which really caught on (Tac. *Agr.* 18. 6; Suet. *Cal.* 31). *Fortuna*, on the other hand, is a central element of imperial ideology, and this passage is possibly the first reference to Octavian's Fortune (cf. the fascinating historical survey at Plin. *NH* 7. 147 ff. with R. Till, *Würz. Jhb.* 3 (1977), 128 ff.): Suet. *Aug.* 94. 1 talks about his continuous good fortune; cf. too Plut. *Fort. Rom.* 7 (= Plut. *Mor.* (Loeb edn.), 4. 340 ff.).

19. 4. as a girl. Caecilia was forced to divorce in 28 on Agrippa's marriage to Marcella; what happened to her then is unknown. Vipsania Agrippina need not have been her only child; cf. M. Reinhold, *CPh* 67 (1972), 119 ff. for the possibility of another daughter who married P. Quinctilius Varus.

Drusilla. It is not quite clear (cf. note on 12. 2, **marriage**) when Caecilia married or, therefore, when Vipsania Agrippina was born; her early engagement to Tiberius (born 42) was his mother Livia's doing (Syme (1939), 345); note N. calls her 'Drusilla'. Their child was Drusus the younger, born 13 BC, who was embarrassed by his equestrian origins (Tac. *Ann.* 2. 43. 7). Tiberius was forced to divorce in order to marry Julia, Augustus' own daughter (11 BC; D.C. 54. 35. 4). He was very fond of Vipsania and she was pregnant again at the time of her divorce (Suet. *Tib.* 7. 2 f.; D.C. 54. 31. 2). She later married a son of Asinius Pollio the historian and became the mother of several consuls by him (Reinhold, *Marcus Agrippa*, 137; Tac. *Ann.* 1. 12. 6, 6. 23. 3, 4. 61. 1; D.C. 57. 2. 7, 60. 27. 5). She died in 20 AD, the only child of Agrippa to meet a natural death, according to Tacitus (*Ann.* 3. 19. 4 f.).

this . . . frequent. 'Link' translates 'coniunctio'; cf. Cic. *Off.* 1. 11. Hellegouarc'h (1963), 81 f. notes that it is used particularly of political alliances. 'Close relations' ('necessitudo'), is used particularly of intimate association (Hellegouarc'h (1963), 71 ff.). 'Friendly intercourse' is 'familiaritas', more or less equivalent to 'amicitia' (cf. note on 13. 7, **this . . . relations**), with a hint of regular contact (Hellegouarc'h (1963), 68 f.).

20. 1. friend or kinsman. Simply 'sui', 'his', which can denote either: cf. Hor. *Serm.* 2. 6. 41 'suorum in numero', of the point at which Maecenas admits Horace to the limited number of his intimates; Catul. 58. 3, 72. 4; and the proverb quoted at Petr. 43. 5 'he flees far who flees his' ('longe fugit quisquis suos fugit').

word. Many fragments of Augustus' letters survive (best consulted in the edition by H. Malcovati of the fragments of Augustus (Turin 1944, etc.)); cf. too H. Bardon, *Les Empereurs et la littérature latine* (Paris 1940), 33 ff. Suetonius was able (*Aug.* 71, 87; cf. Wallace-Hadrill (1983), 91 ff.) to consult many in autograph in the imperial archives; others were apparently available in published versions.

reading. Suetonius (*Aug.* 89) records that he looked especially for 'precepts and examples' in Greek and Latin, which he sent to the relevant magistrates; he even read out and publicized entire speeches. Cf. note on 19. 2 (**he . . . state**) for his intentions in so doing.

20. 2. enjoyed. Cf. note on 4. 2 (**Italy**) for the pleasure taken by Roman *principes* from Sulla to Augustus (and the span could be extended) in educated companions; cf. also P. White in B. K. Gold (ed.), *Literary and Artistic Patronage in Ancient Rome*, (Austin 1982), 50 ff.

antiquity. It is interesting that Octavian did not consult M. Terentius Varro, ten years Atticus' senior, but still intellectually active, and (cf. note on 18. 1, **antiquity**) perhaps even too full of information. At just this date Horace (*Serm.* 2. 2. 103–4) asks why the ancient temples of the gods are crumbling when rich men have money to spare. The atrium Libertatis, Regia, temple of Hercules Musarum, temple of Aventine Diana, and perhaps the hut of Romulus were all rebuilt in the ten years before Actium. Antiquarian patriotism is not an Augustan invention; its scholarly origins go back (chapter 18) to the Caesarian period, and the idea that victorious generals should spend some of their profits on the restoration of temples belongs to the triumviral period as a whole (cf. F. W. Shipley, *MAAR* 9 (1931), 7 ff.; Horsfall, *Vergilius* 32 (1986), 9 ff.).

poetry. Octavian wrote a little poetry himself (Suet. *Aug.* 85) and energetically disliked archaizers (ib. 86). Some fragments survive (cf. Malcovati's ed., supra) and others were attributed to him (Bardon, *Les Empereurs*, 14 ff.). N.'s hint at the seriousness of Octavian's literary interests, even at critical times in his career, is amply confirmed by Suetonius (*Aug.* 84 ff.).

coaxed. Much the terms in which Suetonius' life of Horace misrepresents the circumstances under which Horace composed *Ep.* 2. 1 (cf. E. Fraenkel, *Horace* (Oxford 1957), 17 ff.). Suetonius there preserves some verbatim specimens of imperial arm-twisting. Augustus used a similar tone to Virgil, requesting some token of work in progress (on the *Aeneid* see Suet.–Don., *Vita* 31) and J. Griffin in F. Millar and E. Segal, (eds.), *Caesar Augustus* (Oxford 1984), 202 f. We really do not know if we exaggerate the 'bullying' tone.

20. 3. Jupiter Feretrius. Cf. Platner–Ashby, *Topographical Dictionary*, s.v. *Iuppiter Feretrius*. The temple was probably within the precinct of the temple of Jupiter Capitolinus, to the right as you climb the modern staircase to the Capitol and behind the Museo dei Conservatori.

founded by Romulus. The first temple consecrated at Rome—to commemorate the winning of the *spolia opima* ('the rich spoils') when he in person killed Acron, king of the Caeninenses (Liv. 1. 10. 5, 7 with Ogilvie's notes and Verg. *Aen.* 6. 855–9 with Austin's excellent discussion).

restoration. The first on the list of temples Augustus restored at *RG* 12 (where there is no word, of course, of Atticus). 'He restored it when it had collapsed through age' says Livy (4. 20. 7); Livy had heard that Octavian (as he was then) had gone in and read the inscription on the corselet of A. Cornelius Cossus, second winner of the *spolia opima* (437 BC; cf. previous note). He claimed thereafter (untenably!) that he had documentary evidence that Cossus had won the *spolia* as consul and that therefore M. Licinius Crassus, merely proconsul of Macedonia and in consequence not holding full *imperium*, was not entitled to them for killing Deldo the Bastarnian with his own hands (this is the qualifying deed) in 29 (cf. Ogilvie on Livy, loc. cit.; R. Syme, *HSCP* 64 (1959), 43 ff. = *Roman Papers*, i (1979), 417 ff.). The episode, from which Livy emerges with credit and Augustus without, shows that antiquarian research at this date did also matter in the real world.

20. 4. no less. Cf. 12. 2 with notes; N. refers, that is, both in the first (35–32 BC) and the second edition (32–27) to Atticus' good relations with Mark Antony, though here he does not trouble to mention the fact in tones of hushed embarrassment, which might have been expected at this date.

lands. From Philippi (42) to the Treaty of Brundisum (40), from 39 to the Treaty of Tarentum (37), and from 37 till his death Antony was in the East.

20. 5. reader. We do not know the circumstances in which a second edition was published, nor who the dedicatee of the *Latin Historians* was, except (p. 8) that it was probably not Atticus; N. here, like Livy (*Praef.* 9), Virgil (*G.* 1. 498 ff.), and Horace (*Epode* 7) appeals to his readers' shared participation in the tensions and horrors of the 30s (Jal (1963), 231 ff.).

leading man. A most significant text in the shift from 'a *princeps*', or magnate or leading man, in republican terms (such as Horace still uses at *Carm.* 4. 14. 6, when he calls Augustus 'greatest of *principes*') to 'the *princeps*', or single leading man of the Roman world (Syme (1939), 288, 311, 519; Hellegouarc'h (1963), 358); cf. Gelzer (1969), 44 ff. for the republican usage. N.'s distant and just appraisal of the late 30s as a personal power-struggle between Antony and Octavian is at this date (cf. note on 20. 4, **no less**) striking.

insults. 'Obtrectatio tanta' I translate as 'such an exchange of insults' (as indeed took place—often studied: Syme (1939), 276 ff.; N. Mackie, in *Studies in Latin Literature* 4, C. Deroux (ed.) *Coll. Lat.* 196 (1986), 302 ff); so too 5, 4 (none between Cicero and Hortensius), and *Eum.* 10. 2. The difficulty is, though, that if N.'s word order is respected closely, it commits us to construing 'highest prizes' with both 'exchange of insults' and (much easier) with 'competition'. I do not know what 'maximarum rerum obtrectatio' taken together should mean. Easier, then, to suggest a flawed sentence-structure and translate as I have done.

of the world. Cf. note on 20. 5 (**leading man**).

21. 1. influence. Cf. 2. 4 'The charm which was already abundant when he was a young man' and 6. 2 'he sought no offices, though they lay open to him through both his influence and his standing' (the same pair). For *dignitas*, a word used repeatedly by N. of Atticus, (cf. note on 2. 2, **standing**; *gratia* is here used clearly as 'influence', not 'charm'; though *gratia* and *dignitas* can be polarized (*gratia* is what fortune brings you, *dignitas* comes from your virtues; cf. Cic. *Marc.* 19, *Mur.* 17), they are also often used as near-synonyms. N., therefore, refers here to Atticus' standing in society and the influence he can in consequence exert (cf. Gelzer (1969),

75 f.; Wistrand (1978), 12; Hellegouarc'h (1963), 363, 399; C. Moussy, *Gratia* (Paris 1966), 385).

inheritances. Two inheritants were mentioned in chapter 14; neither was very large, though they are essential to N.'s presentation of the sources of Atticus' wealth (cf. note on 14. 3, **income**); here at last he indicates that there were others. Legacies and inheritances were a standard source of income (cf. Shatzman (1975), 50 ff.). Atticus' beneficiaries would be expected to recall the 'officia' (cf. note on 4. 2, **sense of duty**) performed on their behalf (many of which, at least in theory, were supposed to be gratuitous), to assess their value, and remember him (cf. note on 11. 5, **grateful**) in appropriate terms. Cf. Saller (1982), 25 ff., 122 ff.; Brunt (1965), 7 = Seager (1969), 205; Wistrand (1978), 12 ff.

medicine. Doctors (many of them Greek), and medicine at Rome have attracted much attention recently: avoid J. Scarborough, *Roman Medicine* (London 1969), but cf. (e.g.) Rawson (1985), 170 ff.; D. Gourevitch *Le Triangle hippocratique* (Rome 1984).

fell ill. 'Deaths of distinguished men' are an elaborate literary form; last scenes develop from Plato's account of Socrates' end down to the copious literature about the younger Cato's suicide (he read the *Phaedo* twice during his last night). We have noted elsewhere the possibility that the Cato literature may have been indirectly influential upon N. (see, e.g., note on *Cato*, 3. 5, **Atticus**); we shall see (note on 22. 1, **one ... another**) that N. quoted (unmistakeably) the *Phaedo*! Cf. M. Griffin, *G&R* 33 (1986), 202; S. J. Harrison, *CQ* 36 (1986), 505 f.

21. 2. bowel. 'Tenesmos' proved too difficult for commentators on N. hitherto, but there is no problem at all; *OED* s.v. gives 'continual inclination to void with straining but little or no discharge', and that is precisely the ancient sense as given in Plin. *NH* 28. 211 and Cels. 4. 25. 2.

21. 3. treatment. Pliny, loc. cit., gives remedies (cf. also Scrib. Larg. 142, Cels. loc. cit.): drinking cow's or ass's milk, sitting in hot water, drinking butter in rosewater, or water and a light dry wine on alternate days ...

loins. The word *lumbi*, rather like 'loins', is wonderfully imprecise (cf. J. N. Adams, *Latin Sexual Vocabulary* (London 1982), 48).

21. 4. summoned. Griffin *G&R*, 33, 64 f., 198, speaks of the 'theatricality', the 'social character', the 'staging' of Roman suicides (cf. Tac. *Ann.* 15. 62 on Seneca, Plin. *Ep.* 1. 12 on Corellius); cf. R. MacMullen, *Enemies of the Roman Order* (Cambridge, Mass. 1966), 46 ff. Cf. Val. Max. 2. 6. 8 on the town of Iulis on Ceos, where an old lady had to render account to her fellow citizens of her motives for wanting to die.

Lucius . . . him. N. refers probably to L. Cornelius Balbus of Gades (Cadiz), made a Roman citizen in 72, but not a senator before his suffect consulship (the first foreign consul) of 40. A very wealthy supporter of Caesar and Octavian. Friend of Cicero, Varro, and Atticus; author of *Ephemerides* (a sort of diary), reader of Cic. *Fin.* 5 before publication, and dedicatee of Hirtius' eighth book of the *Gallic War* (completing Caesar's account). It is uncertain when he died; N. could in theory be speaking of his homonymous nephew. Cf. Shatzman (1975), 329 f.; Wiseman (1971), 21 f. Peducaeus is a son of the man who was praetor in Sicily when Cicero was quaestor (75); probably neither tribune in 55 nor governor of Sardinia in 48 (SB i. 34). Cicero pays tribute to the 'humanitas' (cf. note on 4. 1, **captured**) and 'probitas' of both father and son (*Fin.* 2. 58); there is notable cordiality in Cicero's references to him (*Att.* 10. 1. 1 (his father, here, too); ibid. 15. 13. 3, 16. 11. 1, 16. 15. 4). The evidence in *MRR* ii. 385 does not permit the construction of any sort of public career that will hold up. We might wonder whether N. was present at Atticus' death (cf. Geiger (1985), 109); perhaps we should expect him to say so if he had been. But I rather doubt that he was close enough to Atticus to have been asked. As it is, a witness will have told him; both Balbus and Peducaeus will have known well the mould in which such accounts should be cast, as indeed N. clearly did himself. Atticus (21. 5) leaned on one elbow to speak; quite natural, one might suppose, but a detail not, apparently, found earlier; the old lady of Ceos did so (see note on 21. 6, **dissuasion**; Val. Max. 2. 6. 8); likewise, Virgil's Dido (*Aen.* 4. 690); the detail then swiftly becomes a conventional ornament in the poets (cf. Bömer's note on Ov. *Met.* 7. 347). It is clearly not relevant that that is how river gods are often portrayed; more to the point, the detail is quite characteristic of banqueting scenes of a funerary or heroic character in art (R. M. Gais, *AJA* 82 (1978), 363). Did N. also have in his mind a picture of how the scene *ought* to look?

21. 5. health. Socrates, said Seneca (*Ep.* 70. 9), could have died more quickly by voluntary starvation; that was how the philosopher Cleanthes died (Diog. Laert. 7. 176); cf. Griffin, *G&R* 33, 70, 74; Y.

Grisé, *Le Suicide dans la Rome antique* (Paris 1982), 68 f.; etc. The care
and attention which Atticus claims he has exercised is so characteristic: 9. 4, 4. 3, 13. 4, 13. 5, 18. 1; cf. 21. 3.

own interests. Had Atticus been a Stoic, prolonged and severe pain
would have been thought a sufficient argument for suicide (cf.
Griffin, *G&R* 33, 73; Sen. *Ep.* 58. 32 ff., 77. 6; Plin. *Ep.* 1. 12, 1. 22.
8), outweighing his duties to family and friends. The Epicurean
position was a good deal more complicated (Griffin, *G&R* 33, 67,
72): Atticus could be expected to have rid himself of irrational fears
of death, and hence, on the Epicurean view, of despair of life as well.
But that was not sufficient to exclude the legitimacy of suicide, if the
pain of an illness was sufficient utterly to negate what they believed
to be the *summum bonum* of life, pleasure (Cic. *Fin.* 1., 41, 49, 62; Sen.
De vita beata 19. 1). Not a word, though, of Epicureanism in N.'s
account (nor is there when he writes of Saufeius and Lucretius); cf.
Griffin, *G&R* 33, 67, 76 n. 6. Did Atticus, asks Griffin, not mention
his creed because his end was unorthodox? Or did N. 'edit it out'
because he had no time for philosophy? It is also significant that (cf.
note on 17. 3, **philosophers**) Atticus' Epicureanism was not at all
intense; he was at the same time seriously interested in the Academy
(see notes on 2. 2, and 12. 3, **philosophy**) and N. actually imports
one strong Platonist echo (see note on 22. 1, **one another**). Further,
Atticus' 'resolve' (22. 1, 'constantia'), notes Griffin (76 n. 7), is
rather Stoic! Serious ethical thought was not the monopoly of any
one school and there was a surprising amount of common ground
between the philosophies (as is, or should be, clear to students of
Horace, particularly in the *Epistles* (cf. 1. 1. 13 ff.; Macleod (1983),
225 ff.); the Stoic Cato did not, after all, read Cleanthes twice on his
last night on earth. I suggest, then, that Atticus' last words will have
been characteristically neutral and elusive, and that what specific
philosophy there was will have been further toned down by N.,
hostile if not deaf (p. 13).

21. 6. pain without hope. Cf. Plin. *Ep.* 1. 22. 9, 3. 7. 2 (the poet
Silius Italicus died likewise of an incurable cancer) and indeed, the
example of Epicurus himself (D.L. 10. 15); perhaps only Epicurean
extremists would have questioned Atticus' justification in the
circumstances.

dissuasion. Griffin, *G&R* 33, 66 notes the characteristic calm of the
victim in such scenes; an inheritance from Plato's portrait of
Socrates' last hours. So Cato in the face of attempts to deter (Plut.
Cat. Min. 69. 1): 'now I am my own master' (cf. 21. 5 'all that is left

is that I now look after my own interests'!) similarly Sextus
Pompeius tries to dissuade the old lady of Ceos (Val. Max. 2. 6. 8);
also, we may compare Regulus moving aside his kinsmen as they try
to block his departure for Carthage and the certainty of a terrible
death (Hor. *Carm.* 3. 5. 51 f.; not noted by Harrison in his useful
remarks on that poem and the *Atticus*, *CQ* 36 (1986), 504–7); the
attempts of Corellius' family and friends to dissuade him are
positively macabre (Plin. *Ep.* 1. 12; cf. 1. 22. 8 ff.). The interlocutors
not only contribute to the public, almost 'ceremonial', character of
the death-scene, but their attempts at dissuasion elicit an element of
philosophical dialogue as the 'victim' is compelled to marshal his
counter-arguments.

22. 1. one ... another. The image of 'moving house', not attributed
to Atticus, but a comment by N., is found in Plato (*Phd.* 61d etc.)
and is then taken up by Cicero (*Rep.* 6. 15, *Tusc.* 1. 97, etc.); cf. too
Cic. *Fin.* 1. 49 'like leaving the theatre'; cf. Harrison, *CQ* 36, 505;
Griffin, *G&R* 33, 76 n. 7.

22. 2. begged. Cf. note on 21. 6 (**dissuasion**).

dearest to him. For the arguments used to make Atticus change his
mind the closest parallel is to be found in those used by the family
council to Corellius (Plin. *Ep.* 1. 12; Griffin, *G&R* 33, 66 f.).

22. 3. bearable. The illness is clearly some sort of cancer of the
lower bowel; cf. Gourevitch, *Le Triangle hippocratique*, p. 480.

fifth ... consuls. Such precise detail befits the founder of Roman
historical chronology.

22. 4. directed. The modesty of the funeral is clearly in keeping
with Atticus' general self-restraint and frugality (chapter 13). It was
normal for details to be prescribed in the will (Hopkins (1983),
205 f.; Petr. 71. 5 ff.); funerals could often be elaborate and costly,
and the expenditure might be huge (Hopkins (1983), 206; Petr. 42.
6; Toynbee (1971), 54 for attempts to restrict).

without . . . procession. Likewise no ceremony in the case of
Seneca, as prescribed in his will (Tac. *Ann.* 15. 64. 5). On the
procession cf. Toynbee (1971), 46 ff.; the ceremonial details of a
senatorial funeral had been minutely described by Polybius 6. 53–4.
Public funerals had become occasions for the display of intense
popular sentiment (Nicolet (1980), 346 ff.). Atticus ensures that the

arrangements are typically modest, but—no surprise—a huge crowd testifies to the affection he inspired (cf. 4. 5).

men of substance. Cf. note on 6. 1 (**optimates**); for the popular reaction cf. his departure from Athens (4. 5).

fifth milestone. Burials took place outside the limits of the city, originally for reasons of hygiene; numerous tombs and fragments of tombs can still be seen along the Appian Way. Cf. Hopkins (1983), 205; Toynbee (1971), 48, 73.

tomb . . . uncle. On families buried in the same grave cf. the extreme case of the Scipiones (Toynbee (1971), 103 ff.; J. van Sickle, *AJPh* 108 (1987), 41 ff.). Given Atticus' relations with his uncle, and the legacy he received in consequence (5. 1–2), along with 'testamentary adoption' (see note on 5. 2, **three-quarters**), it seems curiously appropriate that the two old moneylenders were buried together.

PROLOGUE TO THE LIVES OF THE FOREIGN GENERALS

For an introduction to this *Prologue* see pp. xix–xxi. T. Janson's valuable *Latin Prose Prefaces* (Stockholm 1964) demonstrates the persistence of conventional, inherited elements in such texts. He mysteriously omits N., but several commonplaces are discussed below (see note on 8, **haste**).

1. Atticus. He was, then, the recipient at least of this book, but (see p. 8) certainly not of the whole *Vitae*.

that . . . men. Clearly no dispraise of biography in general is intended (Geiger (1985), 113, rightly, against Horsfall, *CHCL* ii. 291); N. acknowledges rather the likelihood that criticism will be levelled at the inconcinnity between 'frivolous' personal information and the dignity of the great men whose lives he is writing.

music. Cf. Nep. *Epam*. 2. 1; Epaminondas was a Theban statesman and soldier, d. 362 BC; 'perhaps the greatest of the Greeks . . . he sang splendidly to the lyre, while Themistocles some years earlier refused to take up the lyre and was considered rather ignorant' (Cic. *Tusc*. 1. 4, tr. A. E. Douglas); cf. Petrochilos (1974), 174.

pipes. At Rome musical education was in general not esteemed as highly as in Greece (but cf. note on Cato, fr. 118, banqueting songs): distinctions between children and adults, public and private, men and women, amateurs (Romans) and professionals (Greeks), aristocrats and others in practice operated, but an element of prejudice existed to which N., Cicero (*Pis*. 22, *Mur*. 13), and Cato the Elder (*Orat*. fr. 115 = Macr. *Sat*. 3. 14. 9) might all appeal. Cf. Balsdon (1962), 274 f.; id., (1969), 152; Petrochilos (1974), 172 ff.; Bonner (1977), 44; Sall. *Cat*. 25. 2 with McGushin's note; Rawson (1985), 167 ff.

2. literature. Cf. Nep. *Pel*. 1. 1 and pp. xix–xxi for N.'s monoglot, middlebrow public.

morality. Cf. H. Baldry (1965), 194 ff. for Cicero (e.g. *Leg*. 1. 32 on the unimportance of religious differences); Str. 1. 4. 9 cites Eratosthenes on good barbarians and bad Greeks. But high-minded theory foundered repeatedly on manifold and ineradicable prejudice: Balsdon (1979), 64 ff., 214 ff.; H. Baldry in *Entr. Fond. Hardt*, 8 (1961), 191; Rawson (1985), 262 f. on Caesar's reluctance to judge Gauls and Germans.

3. practice. Cf. Cic. *Tusc.* 5. 78 for variation in funeral rites. The language is strongly reminiscent of Cicero: *Rep.* 1. 71, *Sest.* 140, *Am.* 40. For the implicit belief in law (as against nature) see Guthrie (1969), 55 ff.

standards. For the origins (Herodotus, Euripides) of these enlightened views cf. Guthrie (1969), 16 ff., 317. Cf. Nep. *Ham.* 3. 2 for tolerance of Carthaginian mores and *Dat.* 5. 4 for awareness of Persian ways.

4. half-sister. Cf. Nep. *Cim.* 1. 2; Plut. *Cim.* 4. 8; not just a half-sister, according to Cimon's detractors (Davies (1971), 303).

same practice. Cf. Lacey (1968), 106 for Greek marriage to half-sisters, and Stevens on E. *Andr.* 173 ff. for further Greek references to incest among the barbarians.

outrage. For 'prohibited degrees' at Rome cf. Watson (1967), 38 f.; for uncles and nieces cf. Hallett (1984), 159 f. (not normally acceptable). The imperial family made its own rules (Balsdon (1962), index s.v. *incest*).

In . . . impossible. Indeed Cicero suggeseted that it was a reproach if they did not (*Rep.* 4. 3); cf. Ephorus, *FGH* 70 F 149 = Str. 10. 4. 21; Marrou (1956), 28; Willetts (1965), 115 f.; Dover (1980), 189 f.

There . . . fee. It is likely, but not certain, that N. wrote 'cenam', 'dinner' (cf. H. Malcovati, *Athen.* 55 (1977), 418): if so, we have no notion of what he was trying to say (Michell (1952), 50 f.). But Sparta's many wars and few whores created endemic oddities in sexual mores (Rawson (1969), 94 ff.; Lacey (1968), 199). Sparta could ill afford to waste fecund women (see Plut. *Cleom.* 6; Plb. 12. 6. 5); even 'widow' is not quite certain; the word could refer to a woman whose husband was at war. But Romans well knew how correct a polite Greek dinner was (Cic. *Verr.* 2. 1. 66).

5. victor at Olympia. Horace (*Carm.* 1. 1. 3 ff.) similarly places Olympic victory first in his catalogue of human goals (see the commentary of R. G. M. Nisbet and M. E. Hubbard); cf. further M. I. Finley and H. W. Pleket, *The Olympic Games* (London 1976).

to ... populace. Actors' privileges accumulated especially from the fourth century BC on (e.g. exemption from military service, honorific statues, sent on diplomatic missions): see G. M. Sifakis, *Studies in the History of Hellenistic Drama* (London 1967); A. Pickard-Cambridge, *Dramatic Festivals of Athens*^{2} (Oxford 1968), 279 ff. There is some improvement in the status of actors at Rome in the course of the first century BC, while restrictions against public performance by senators and knights grow ever tighter; cf. Horsfall, *CHCL* ii. 293 ff.; id. *BICS* 23 (1976), 81; B. Levick, *JRS* 73 (1983), 105 ff.; Rawson (1985), 152. The contrast with Greece is familiar (Cic. *Rep.* 4. 11 f., 4. 13; Liv. 24. 24. 3; Petrochilos (1974), 176). Greek gymnastics aroused mixed admiration and contempt; Petrochilos (1974), 177 f.; Balsdon (1969), 162 f.; H. A. Harris, *Sport in Greece and Rome* (London 1972), 44 ff.; cf. e.g. Cic. *de Orat.* 2. 20–21 *passim*. On attitudes to Greek homosexuality (cf. Nep. *Alc.* 2. 2; Cic. *Tusc.* 4. 70 f., *Rep.* 4. 4) cf. Petrochilos (1974), 181 f.; Balsdon (1979), 225 ff.; Griffin (1985), 24 ff.; R. MacMullen, *Hist.* 31 (1982), 484 ff.

6. dinner party. Cf. Ov. *Am.* 1. 4: some Romans might have preferred not to take their wives out to dinner! Cf. Balsdon (1962), 277; Friedlaender, i. 248.

guests. Traditionally the Roman matron ate, wove, worshipped, cooked, and slept in the atrium; at least in conservative households in N.'s time they still sat at dinner (Val. Max. 2. 1. 2).

7. family. Older books on women in the Greek world greatly exaggerate the seclusion of Greek women; cf. rather Lacey (1968) and Pomeroy (1975) against (e.g.) W. A. Becker, *Charicles* (Eng. tr., London 1895), 472.

women's quarters. N. understood the matter no better than Becker: cf. Lacey (1968), 168 f.; Pomeroy (1975), 80 f., and the classic exposition of A. W. Gomme, *Essays in Greek Literature and History* (Oxford 1937), 89 ff. for a more balanced picture.

8. scale. *Foreign Generals* is the longest single book in classical Latin literature (Horsfall, *CHCL* ii. (1982) 292; Geiger (1985), 85), and is but one book out of (?) 18 (Geiger (1985), 92) in the work as a whole; cf. Liv. 31. 1. 1.

haste. On the many prefatory references to haste cf. Janson, *Latin Prose Prefaces*, 96; A. J. Woodman, *CQ* 25 (1975), 275 ff. (e.g. Var. *RR* 1. 1; Verg. *G.* 4. 117; Hor. *Ep.* 2. 1. 1 f.); N. does not, like an epitomator, or Velleius, aim explicitly at brevity, but the work's colossal scale presupposes omissive treatment!

NEPOS: SELECTED FRAGMENTS

Chronica

2. The fragments of the *Chronica* give of themselves little idea of what might have aroused Catullus, who writes in the brief period between the appearance of N.'s book and its virtual supersession by Atticus' *Liber annalis* (cf. note on *Att.* 18. 1, **volume . . . order**): Douglas (1966), p. lii; Geiger (1985), 68 f. N. is a fellow Transpadane (cf. Wiseman (1985), 108 ff.) and himself a writer of minor erotic verse (Plin. *Ep.* 5. 3. 6). He was twenty-five years Catullus' senior, a protégé of Atticus, and an acquaintance of Cicero (cf. pp. xvi). Nothing there that clamours for a dedication in return. Geiger (1985), 68 and.Wiseman (1979), 170 f. do not altogether convince me that Catullus' tone is one of sincere admiration, untainted by any flicker of humour at the expense of N.'s praiseworthy industry. But he may have been genuinely attracted by the Greek genre, title, and learning of the *Chronica* (cf. Wiseman (1979), 157 ff.; id. (1985), 197; Geiger (1985), 68 ff.; Rawson (1985), 103). A conscientious attempt to synchronize the political and intellectual histories of Greece and Rome (which had not been done before) must, however prolix and confused, have been something of a revelation to a writer immersed in Greek literature as Catullus was: even if not a miracle of erudite prose in Latin (as is sometimes now claimed: cf. F. Decreus, *Lat.* 43 (1984), 842 ff.), possibly fascinating and deserving of a compliment in return. And N. went on in turn to compliment Catullus (cf. notes on *Att.* 12. 4).

4. Cicero (*Rep.* 2. 18) and many Roman historians depend on N., who in turn follows Apollodorus' *Chronica*. The date given for Homer (914) is in today's view far too early; more important, N., who gives 914/13 in lieu of 944/3 has either confused Homer's floruit with his death, or more probably equated Lycurgus' floruit with his legislation, with consequent variation from Apollodorus on Homer's date (Fantham (1981), 8, 13 f. and, above all, Jacoby, *FGH* 2 D p. 747).

6. Not conclusively N.; Sex. Julius Africanus' catalogue of Olympic victors (Eusebius, *Chronica*, ed. Schoene, 1. 201 f.) confirms only that he won a victory in 532; cf. Paus. 6. 14. 2 f. with Frazer's notes.

7. King Tullus reigned 673–42; we would say that Archilochus flourished about 650. An improvement over Cic. *Tusc.* 1. 3 after Varro, who dates Archilochus to the reign of Romulus; Fantham, 8.

8. For the problems of Gauls' route, the identification of the Tarpeian rock, and indeed the date of the Gallic siege cf. Bremmer and Horsfall (1987), 63 ff.; Wiseman (1979), 36. N.'s version is confirmed by an alternative account cited by Liv. 6. 20. 12 ('some say that he was condemned by the duoviri created to take cognizance of crime against the state'); these two accounts appear correct against the great mass of the rest of the tradition, since flogging was the correct punishment for *perduellio*, and the *duoviri* of Livy loc. cit. are likewise the correct magistrates to act in such circumstances. Cf. E. Rawson, *CQ* 37 (1987), 175 f.

9. The consular date is 354; Alexander was born in 356. The foundation N., after Eratosthenes, placed in the second year of the seventh Olympiad, i.e. 751/0 (see fr. 5, Solin. 1. 27). Atticus and Cicero (ibid.) preferred 754/3 (Ol. 6. 3). Varro likewise: cf. Censorinus 21. 6; we need to remember that Rome was traditionally founded on 21 April, towards, that is, the end of the Olympic year 754/3. Cf. further p. 100 for Atticus' foundation date and for the synchronism of AUC and consular dates; also Bickerman (1968), 77.

37. N. does not merit Gellius' first compliment; that is objectively demonstrable; the friendship with Cicero (but cf. J. Geiger, *Lat.* 44 (1985), 261 f.) seems a good deal overstated (cf. fr. 39). Cicero was born in 106 and the case took place in 80; cf. e.g. Mitchell (1979), 90 ff. N. presumably knew the date of birth; either his arithmetic or (more probably) his legal chronology is at fault.

38. The first trace of the young Cisalpine at Rome, listening to the first orator of the day. The speech (lost) was delivered in 65 BC; cf. Kennedy (1972), 276 for the problem of 'published versions'.

Letters

39. Cf. J. Geiger, *Lat.* 44 (1985), 264 f.: probably of 45 BC and closely in keeping with what N. says of Atticus at *Att.* 17. 3 (**life**): the value of philosophy was to be seen in life. Cicero complains (*Att.* 16. 5. 5) that N. thinks the works of which he is most proud not worth reading. Cf. Rawson (1985), 95 for hostility to philosophy and Tac. *Agr.* 4. 3 (with Ogilvie's and Richmond's notes) for its classic expression. Was N. the piece of grit in the smooth relations between Atticus and Cicero?

De viris illustribus

54. Terence's *Heautontimorumenos* was performed in 163 BC: so even if there is no truth in the story, it is firmly datable. Laelius is the first Roman noble we know to have built at Puteoli on the Bay of Naples (D'Arms (1970), 6 f.) Cf. Gratwick, *CHCL* ii. 815 on the way stories and rumours grew out of the accusation (which Terence does not deny) that he received help from his noble friends; friends and more according to fr. 53 (Suet. *Poet.* 6. 1, in the Loeb edition of Suetonius, vol. ii). In Terence, a forceful courtesan is speaking and threatening unpunctuality; on the first of March (the Matronalia), Laelius, 'the Wise' might have been expected not to keep his wife waiting.

56. The Greek historian Polybius (39. 1. 1 f.; see Walbank's note) preserves the same retort (cf. Horsfall, *EMC* 23 (1979), 87; Kaimio (1979), 228 f.). Cato was indeed the first Roman historian to write in Latin; his predecessors had like Albinus used Greek. Was this from a life of Albinus or from the longer version (cf. note on *Cato*, 3. 5, **separate study**) of the life of Cato? For Cato's anti-Hellenism cf. notes on *Cato*, 3. 2 (**older man** and **Greek . . . affairs**) and Astin (1978), 168 f. with the critique of E. Rawson, *JRS* 70 (1980), 198 f. On this episode cf. further Badian (1966), 6 f.; Petrochilos (1974), 164 f.; Horsfall, *EMC* 23 (1979), 87; Kaimio (1979), 228.

57. The Sullan annalists (Quadrigarius, and arguably Antias too) were likewise not of senatorial family. The very name and elements in the biography of Voltacilius are unclear (Rawson (1985), 79, 91). He was not the only writer (cf. Theophanes) to celebrate the glory of the Pompeii, on the ever-present model of Alexander; cf. Rawson (1985), 92. For Pompey as public speaker cf. Cic. *Brut.* 239; he resumed declamation just before the civil war (Suet. *Rhet.* 3); cf. further Kennedy (1972), 282.

58. For the provenance of this excerpt see P. K. Marshall, *The Manuscript Tradition of Cornelius Nepos, BICS* Suppl. 37 (1977), 8 f. For the deficiencies of philosophy in Latin before Cicero cf. p. xxi and Rawson (1985), 285. Cicero was a serious student of the theory of history, as a scholar often concerned with historical problems, and as Livy's potential, unfulfilled predecessor has attracted a good deal of attention: Rawson (1985), 217 and *JRS* 62 (1972), 43; Petrochilos

(1974), 156; J. Geiger, *Lat.* 44 (1985), 266f.; P. G. Walsh, *Livy* (1961), 33f.; P. A. Brunt, *Miscellanea in onore di Eugenio Manni*, i (Rome 1979), 311ff.

61. This 'libellus' of N. remains a complete mystery; we may regret the loss of distinctions drawn by a man who will have had some idea of the real difference between Atticus and Varro, and between Cicero and either of them. For the terminological problems cf. Bonner (1977), 55f.; M. L. Clarke, *Higher Education in the Ancient World* (1971), 21; E. W. Bower, *Herm.* 89 (1961), 462ff.; A. D. Booth, *Herm.* 109 (1981), 371ff.

62. This may be from the *Exempla*, not a life; cf. p. xvii–xviii for *Exempla*. Cf. note on *Att.* 9. 1 (**Modena**).

CATO: SELECTED FRAGMENTS

Origines

1–3. Three scraps from the *proemium*: cf. Badian (1966), 8; Astin (1978), 221 f. Cf. fr. 77 and Nepos, fr. 56 for other views of Cato on the writing of history; his predecessors had written either in Greek (e.g. Fabius Pictor) or in poetry (Naevius). Fr. 2 is an idea drawn by Cato in its present form from the first paragraph of Xenophon's *Symposium*, but expressed and illustrated continuously by Cato (cf. note on *Cato*, 3. 2, **older man** and contrast note on *Att.* 6. 2, **influence and standing** for Atticus' version!). Cf. Sall. *Cat.* 4. 1 and *Jug.* 4.4 for classic expressions of the inherited compulsion to justify *otium* and the writing of history. It is doubtful whether Cic. *Off.* 3. 1 and *Rep.* 1. 27 are relevant to Cato's position here (Astin (1978), 221 n. 32). Note that Cato explains the advantage of history; so Thucydides (1. 22. 4) and Polybius (1. 1. 2 etc.); so too Cato himself on agriculture (*Agr. praef.* 4). Writing about the past, then, is not an end in itself and has like farming a function in life (Astin (1978), 222).

17. Cato, that is, does not calculate (e.g.) by Olympiads, nor does he give synchronisms with Greek events. Though the poets Naevius and Ennius made Romulus a grandson of Aeneas (Skutsch (1985), 190), Cato follows clearly the historians' version: Timaeus dated the fall of Troy between 1346 and 1194/3, Eratosthenes to 1184/3; Fabius Pictor dated the foundation of Rome to 748/7, Timaeus to 814/13. It is likely (Astin (1978), 224) that Cato thought Rome was founded in 751. For these dates cf. H. A. Sanders, *CPh* 3 (1908), 317 ff.; Horsfall, *CQ* 24 (1974), 111 ff.

21. Antemna was situated just downstream of the confluence of the Anio and the Tiber, only three miles from the centre of Rome. The claim is not an uncommon one (cf. fr. 49 on Ameria with Astin (1978), 230 and T. J. Cornell, *PCPhS* 21 (1975), 15 f.); thus too the Julii claimed to have migrated from Alba Longa and Bovillae.

31. Woe betide those Italian peoples who did not keep their records up to date! Cato, like Timaeus, had evidently an appetite for antiquarian fieldwork; cf. fr. 61 on Arpinum with Astin (1978), 231 and Bremmer and Horsfall (1987), 7; also Rawson (1985), 239 *et passim* for his successors.

51. Cf. further fr. 76. The Spartan migration to Sabinum (immediately north-east of Rome) is an explanation in mythological terms of Roman admiration of Sabine austerity and awareness that Sparta furnished the obvious parallel (Rawson (1969), 99 ff.). But it is probable that Servius has garbled Cato's account, which may well be more correctly represented by D.H. 2. 49. 2 f. (J. Poucet in *Études étrusco-italiques* (Louvain 1963), 157 ff.). Cf. further E. Rawson, *Lat.* 35 (1976), 715.

59. All the motifs in this foundation story are common in Indo-European mythological narrative; that does not itself guarantee the story's antiquity and it may be the Praenestines' riposte to Romulus and Remus. Cf. Bremmer and Horsfall (1987), 49 ff., 59 ff.

62. Just how much of this information about the heroine Camilla's father was actually in Cato? Only the Etruscan occupation of Volscian territory, on a careful reading of Servius' note. Archaeologists no longer accept that the Etruscans occupied Volscian territory for long. The name Metabus belongs traditionally to Metapontum, near Taranto, not to Privernum, and it was most probably Virgil who first brought him to Privernum (L. A. Holland, *AJPh* 56 (1935), 212 ff.); Camilla likewise (Horsfall, *CR* 34 (1984), 61 f. and *Athen.* 66 (1988), 31 ff.).

76. An idealization fully expressed at (e.g.) Verg. *G.* 2. 167 ff., 533 ff., *Aen.* 9. 598 ff., 7. 746 ff.; Hor. *Carm.* 3. 6. 37 ff. Cf. Horsfall, *Lat.* 30 (1971), 1108 ff.; R. Thomas, *Lands and Peoples in Roman Poetry*, *PCPhS* Suppl. 7 (1982), 98 ff.; M. Dickie, *PLLS* 5 (1985), 183 ff.: sharply contrasting assessments. We might compare Plut. *Cat. mai.* 20. 6 on how Cato raised his own son.

77. That may also suggest that Cato avoided (cf. Astin (1978), 215) a year-by-year arrangement. Cf. Cic. *De orat.* 2. 52 for another list of the contents: these tables formed the basis, it was supposed (Serv. ad *Aen.* 1. 373) of the *Annales maximi*, whose 'publication' apparently occurred during the Gracchan period (E. Rawson, *Lat.* 35 (1976), 714; but cf. R. M. Ogilvie, *JRS* 71 (1981), 200). Had the *Annales maximi* really contained all that was claimed (Servius says that the names of the consuls and all the magistrates were prefixed and that the *pontifex maximus* was accustomed to record events worthy of note, day by day, at home and on campaign, by sea and by land!), then the Romans could hardly have recorded their early history in the way they have in fact done. The debate on how much of our surviving accounts of early Roman history is essentially credible has recently revived: cf. T. J. Cornell, *JRS* 72 (1982), 203 ff. and in I. Moxon *et al.* (eds.), *Past Perspectives* (1986), 67 ff. against T. P. Wiseman, (1979), 3 ff. and *LCM* 8 (1983), 20 ff. Proponents of 'credibility' are now careful not to exalt 'pontifical tablets', or banqueting songs (cf. note on Cato, fr. 118) or for that matter linen books (R. M. Ogilvie *JRS* 48 (1958), 40 ff.; B. W. Frier, *TAPA* 105 (1975), 79 ff.) into guarantees of reliability. Cf. E. Rawson, *CQ* 21 (1971), 158 ff.; Wiseman (1979), 16 f.; Badian (1966), 1 ff.; and B. W. Frier, *Libri annales pontificum maximum* (Rome 1979), 10 ff. for a history of the debate.

83. Cato recounts the feat of Q. Caedicius, military tribune in the first Punic war, in saving the army of Atilius in a defile near Camarina. His name is variously recorded (cf. *MRR* under 258 BC); is this Cato's fault for electing to give the office. not the name? Livy recounts the same event (22. 60. 11; cf. Front. *Str.* 1. 5. 15). Cf. notes on *Cato*, 3. 4 (**by name**) and Cato, fr. 88 for Cato's omission of names; see note on Cato, frr. 1–3 for the 'function' of history in Cato's view, here well illustrated by the concentration on self-sacrifice in the state's service; cf. Astin (1978), 231 f.

88. It is just possible that a portrait of this elephant survives on a pro-Carthaginian coin from the Val di Chiana (H. H. Scullard, *The Elephant in the Greek and Roman World* (1974), 174); it may also be that Ennius records a joke about him in his verse *Annales* (H. H. Scullard, *CR* 67 (1953), 140 ff.; Skutsch (1985), 687 f.).

95. For Cato's speech cf. Astin (1978), 137 ff. For Servius Galba see note on *Cato*, 3. 4 (**Galba . . . Lusitanians**). See p. 35 for a discussion of Cato's oratory.

118. Cf. Cic. *Brut.* 75. Our testimonia on these songs (gathered, e.g., *HRR* i. 90) agree in limiting the subject-matter to the historical (no myths!); on them once rested an explanation of the transmission and survival of early Roman history (cf. note on Cato, fr. 77 for others!); through Niebuhr's *Roman History*, it inspired Macaulay's *Lays of Ancient Rome*. But the ballad theory has been under heavy attack since 1816 and now lacks respectable exponents. See A. D. Momigliano, *JRS* 47 (1957), 104 ff = *Secondo Contributo* (Rome 1960), 69 ff.; Gratwick, *CHCL* ii. 55.

ATTICUS: SELECTED FRAGMENTS

Liber Annalis

The impact of Atticus' work is best perceived through Cicero (see note on Nep. *Att.* 18. 1, **volume . . . order**).

3. On the events of (?) 494 BC cf. Ogilvie (1965), 381 f.; it was clearly not known when the office of tribune was instituted, and Atticus did not list tribunes (cf. note on *Att.* 18. 2, **For . . . history**).

4. Cf. Liv. 2. 40. 10 for the uncertainty about Coriolanus' death (with Ogilvie's note); for the synchronism of Themistocles and Coriolanus cf. Gell. 17. 21. 11 f., after N.'s *Chronica* (cf. notes on Nepos, frr. 7 and 8). See E. Fantham, *LCM* 6. 1 (1981), 8 and Ogilvie (1965), 315 for the contamination of the stories.

5. What sort of records are meant by *commentarii* we have no idea. The Latin text is uncertain and the subject-matter controversial. Atticus, probably following Varro's *De poetis*, is certainly right, as against the scholar-playwright Accius (170–86), though it is not clear quite why and how Accius went wrong about such relatively recent events (cf. Douglas ad loc. and Gratwick, *CHCL*, ii. 799 ff.).

6. The later Antiochus IV Epiphanes, sent to Rome as one of twenty-six hostages by Antiochus III after his defeat at Magnesia in 190. We find interest in authors' homes in Greek biographies: reflected, e.g., at Gell. 15. 20. 5 (Euripides); N. records (see note on *Att.* 13. 2, **Tamphilus'**) the former owner of Atticus' uncle's house, and Suetonius where Virgil lived (*Vit. Don.* 13).

7. N. lists the claims of 183, 182, and 181; Atticus clarifies the synchronism, left uncertain in the annalists. Cf. Walbank on Plb. 23. 12. 1; Rawson (1985), 246.

8. In 155 BC. The paragraph catalogues Cicero's numerous historical enquiries, in search of background for the *Academica*. We may note that the exact chronology of this embassy, which we think of as a point of exceptional importance in Roman intellectual history (see Astin (1978), 174 ff. for Cato's opposition; cf. note on Nepos, fr. 56) had not been clear even to Cicero. Cf. Sumner (1973), 174 ff.

LETTER OF CORNELIA

A . . . letter. Literally 'words excerpted from'; probably, but not certainly, after N. Born 195–190 BC, youngest daughter of the elder Scipio Africanus and first cousin of Scipio Aemilianus; married Tiberius Sempronius Gracchus, *cos.* 177, 163, *cens.* 169, about 175. Mother of twelve children of allegedly alternating gender, of whom three survived, the tribunes and Sempronia, wife of Scipio Aemilianus. Politics and idealization have encrusted her with colourful circumstantial details. Books on Roman women and the Gracchi do her scant justice, but cf. Bernstein (1978), 42 ff.

historians. Clearly mistaken information: the Gracchi were not historians, and the scribe may have been misled by the MSS headings to the *Cato* and *Atticus*: 'Excerpt from the book of Cornelius Nepos *On the Latin Historians*'. Originally, then, part of *Latin Orators* perhaps, or even (J. Geiger, *Lat.* 38 (1979), 662) *Roman Women*.

The same. The tone of the two excerpts is clearly very different, but the external evidence does not allow us to say that they necessarily came from separate letters.

except . . . Gracchus. He was killed in 133 BC (Bernstein (1978), 220 ff.) on the Capitoline, seeking (perhaps illegally) re-election as tribune. Assailed as he was by senators and their supporters, the actual killers are insignificant; interestingly, the first blow was struck by a fellow tribune, P. Satureius (ibid. 161; E. Badian, *ANRW* i. 1. 723 ff.; Astin (1967), 220 ff.).

enemy. Note that Latin distinguishes firmly between the enemies of an individual ('inimicus', as here) and those of the state ('hostis'), cf. notes on *Att.* 2. 2 (**Cinna**) and 11. 5 (**He . . . avenge**).

children. Cornelia lost her husband very shortly after 153, when Gaius Gracchus was born; it appears that she long survived Gaius' death in 121 but she was apparently dead by 101 (Val. Max. 3. 8. 6).

old age. She was about 70 at the apparent date of the letter.

that . . . it. The English attempts to recapture the confusion of the Latin; the style is, repeatedly, excitable and irregular. That does not prove that the original either was or was not by Cornelia; if it was not, then the author was obliged only to reconstitute the urgency and consequent stylistic lapses that the situation required. These lapses were not then edited out in the various rewritings and perhaps did not strike so infelicitous a stylist as N. as curiously as they do the conscientious editor.

ever. Four successive questions begin massively with 'ecquando', 'whenever'. Unwomanly, it has been thought. But hardly a decisive argument against Cornelia's authorship.

end. Cf. note on **that . . . it** above. The confusion is worse here. Literally, 'shall we ever cease to make an end from trouble, both having and providing them?'.

turmoil and confusion. Acutely spotted (H. U. Istinsky, *Chiron*, 1 (1976), 187 f.) as reflecting the conventional language of the optimates' way of looking at tribunes. Again not decisive against Cornelia's authorship; in so public a letter she could after all herself have used the language of Gaius' enemies.

tribunate. The date (or dramatic date) of the letter is clearly just before Gaius became tribune for the first time in 123.

protector. The interpretation is hotly disputed. Cornelia goes on to reprove her son for leaving her abandoned and deserted, but that probably only indicates his alleged disrespect and disobedience, rather than failure to revere her tutelary 'deus parens', familiar in the plural in a 'Law of Servius Tullius' (Fest. p. 260, 10 L.) and perhaps not unlike the much better-known 'genius'. Cornelia perhaps here more probably expresses an expectation that she will be honoured after her death as a 'deus parens' in family cult, perhaps under the influence of Greek ideas (Weinstock (1971), 295; Ross Taylor (1931), 49).

Then . . . pray. Or is Cornelia excitedly conflating 'to seek the help of the gods' and 'to seek from the gods by means of prayers'? At least the general sense is clear enough.

Index

This index refers to distinguished Romans under the name by which they are most commonly known; thus 'Atticus' not 'Pomponius'. In addition to N., note 'Att'. for Atticus and 'Cic.' for Cicero.

works to Att. 95; career misdated by
N. 118
and anti-Epicurean jokes 98
as historian 119–20
letters of, and N. 94, 96; sequence of 96
readership of philosophical works xxi
relations with N. 91, 94–5, 118–19,
119–20; with Att.; beginnings of 59,
intimacy of 68, in 63 and 58, 66, last
stages of 68, 76, 78; with brother
Quintus 68, in 49, 72, 73; with
Brutus 74; with Hortensius 68–9;
with Lucretius 86
Cicero, Q. Tullius, marriage of 66, 68
as provincial governor 71
relations with brother 73

dating (see also chronology), Roman
methods of, by consuls 48, 65
from foundation of Rome 100
death-scenes 108, 109, 110–11
departures and arrivals of famous men
67
dinner-parties 77, 90
doctors 108
drama, Roman, chronological problems
in 124
Drusilla 104
engaged to Tiberius 99, 104
dying man reclines on elbow 109

education by father at Rome 54, 58
elephants 56, 123
'emperor', use of 103
encomium 110
'enemy', terms for 60, 61, 76, 82, 84, 125
Ennius 50
Epicureanism 13, 97–8
and politics 80, 95, 98
and N. 97
and Stoicism, common ground
between 98
and suicide 110
Epirus 92
equites as jurors 71
as prefects, 71
of long pedigree 58
subdivisions of order 58
and neutrality 69
Esquiline Hill 87
estates, suburban 90, 92
excerpting 47
extortion court 71

Fabii, and Att. 101
family records, unreliability of 109
family trees 100
feuds in public life 53, 82
footmen 89
forgiveness 82
Fortune, blows of 79, 102
N.'s view of 82–3
of Octavian 104
foundation of Rome, date of 100, 118
foundation-stories 55, 122
fractions, at Rome 67
friendship, views of, 12–13
friendship, and shared interests 68
and Epicureanism 98
funeral rites 114
speeches 97
of Att., 111–12
furniture and fittings, standards of 89–90

Gallic sack of Rome 118
games, in Roman politics 50, 51
gardens in ancient Rome 87–8
genealogies, legendary 58
and history 100, 101
gentes Roman, records of 57
gladiators, trade in 92
Gracchi, relations with mother 41–3
gratitude 82–3, 108
graves, family 112
Greek, and Greece, knowledge of at
Rome xix–xx
as spoken by Romans 64–5
use of, by historians at Rome 119
gymnastics, Greek, view of at Rome 115

Hannibal, date of death of 124
Hasdrubal 49
historians, Roman, use of Greek by 119
historiography and the marvellous 57
history, popular interest in, at Rome xxi
writing of, justified 121, 123
Homer, date of, in ancient view 117
house, named after former owner 87
household, slave 88

incest 114
interest, rates of 62, 78
calculation of 67
intolerance 113–14
Italian cities older than Rome 121
Italy, primitive life of, idealized 122
unity of, in Cato 55

names, Roman, full form of, 58
  abbreviated in literary texts 47, 125
  difficulties caused by 51
Naples, bay of, Roman villas on 119
Nepos, Cornelius
  birth and homeland xv; arrival in
    Rome xv, 118; death, 104
  relations with Att. 7, 8, 12, 57, 66, 90–
    1, 109, 113; with Catullus xv, 86,
    117; with Cicero xv, xvi, 94–5, 118–
    19, 119–20; and Lucretius, 86
  sources of, 12–13; echoes Plato 110,
    111; and Xenophon 10, 12; and
    peripatetic biography 10; and
    encomium 10; and Polybius 3; and
    Roman autobiography 10; and
    annalists 4; and Cic.; *Letters* 12, 96,
    Am. 12–13, 68, *Sen.* 3, 13; debt to
    Cic. 12–13, 59, 64; and Att. *Liber
    annalis* 3; reports a view held by Att.
    65, 73
  on Antony xv, 106; on philosophy xvi,
    118; chronology xvii; Cato the elder
    xvii etc.; literary terminology xvii;
    as biographer xvii; and friendship
    12–13; does not mention Cic.'s
    death 73; and contemporary politics
    70; attitudes to Octavian 84, 103,
    104; and Att.'s wealth 91–3; on
    social mobility 103; on realities of
    power 107
  and language used by his subjects 4,
    13, 52, 80; as biographer 10, 11;
    unique accounts in 12; eye for
    significant detail 80; and Greek
    panegyric 82; on Att.'s friendships,
    103
  political views xv, 51, 52, 70, 84;
    moralizing xv, xix, 50, 59, 72, 80,
    103; nose for promising topics xviii;
    defects as scholar and writer xviii, 8;
    as school author xix; knowledge of
    Greek xxi; weaknesses of Life of
    Cato 4, 49, 50, 51, 52, 53; of account
    of Cato, *Origines* 55–7; defects of
    Life of Att. 7, 13, 91, 92–3, 96;
    omissions 12, 92–3; and
    Epicureanism 12, 13; details
    mentioned only by N. 12, 66, 73, 74,
    76, 77; awareness of social change
    58; failure to mention Pilia 65; and
    Epicurean language 73; cites
    Roman proverbs and drama 82–3;

jests 89, 91; humourlessness 91; on
    contemporary events 103;
    reluctance to talk about
    Epicureanism 110; haste of 116;
    errors in *Chronica* 117, 118
  as poet xvii, 117; letters of 118–19;
    audience of xviii, xix–xxi, 62, 113;
    prose style xviii–xix; geographical
    writings xv, xvii; *Chronica* 117–18;
    Exempla xv, xvii–xviii; *De viris
    illustribus* 33–4, 119–20: dating of
    8–9, 102, structure of, 11–12; Lives
    of the Foreign Generals: length 115,
    authorship 47, second edition 7,
    102; *Prologue* xix–xxi, 29–30, 113–
    16; *Lives of the Latin Historians* 3, 8;
    lives of Cato 3, 57; *Cato* 3–6, 47–57;
    Atticus: chronology 8–9, 66, second
    edition 8–9, 107, structure 9,
    chronological detail in 7, 72; Lives
    of Cicero xvi, 3, 125
neutrality, difficulties of 69
  and Epicureanism 80, 85
non-participation in public life 58, 69

Octavian, Nepos' attitude to xv, 83, 103,
    104
  references to 7
  correspondence with Att. 7, 105
  'adoption' of 67; behaves well 80;
    spares Att.'s life 80; and Agrippa's
    marriage 83; Att.'s relations with
    84, 103–5; as *imperator* 103
  sense of history 103, 105, 106; fortune
    of 104
  poetry of 105; letters of 105;
    restoration of temples 105, 106; and
    Livy 107
Olympiads, dating by 121
optimates see Latin terms, s.v.
'oral tradition' 48, 66, 79
Origines, as title 55

'parties' political, at Rome 61, 69, 74–5
patronage, literary 57, 66, 106, 119
pederasty, views of, 114, 115
Peducaeus, Sex. 109
perduellio, punishment for 118
Peripatetic ideas 87
phenomena, natural, in historiography
    57
Philippi, battles of 81